Better Homes and Gardens

step-by-step

wildflowers
& native plants

Peter Loewer

Better Homes and Gardens® Books
Des Moines, Iowa

Better Homes and Gardens® Books
An Imprint of Meredith® Books

Step-by-Step Wildflowers & Native Plants
Senior Editor: Marsha Jahns
Production Manager: Douglas Johnston

Vice President and Editorial Director: Elizabeth P. Rice
Executive Editor: Kay Sanders
Art Director: Ernest Shelton
Managing Editor: Christopher Cavanaugh

President, Book Group: Joseph J. Ward
Vice President, Retail Marketing: Jamie L. Martin
Vice President, Direct Marketing: Timothy Jarrell

Meredith Corporation
Chairman of the Executive Committee: E. T. Meredith III
Chairman of the Board and Chief Executive Officer:
    Jack D. Rehm
President and Chief Operating Officer: William T. Kerr

Produced by ROUNDTABLE PRESS, INC.
Directors: Susan E. Meyer, Marsha Melnick
Executive Editor: Amy T. Jonak
Editorial Director: Anne Halpin
Senior Editor: Jane Mintzer Hoffman
Design: Brian Sisco, Susan Evans, Sisco & Evans, New York
Photo Editor: Marisa Bulzone
Assistant Editor: Alexis Wilson
Assistant Photo Editor: Carol Sattler
Editorial Production: Don Cooper
Encyclopedia Editor: Henry W. Art and Storey
    Communications, Inc., Pownal, Vermont
Horticultural Consultant: Christine M. Douglas
Copy Editors: Sue Heinemann, Virginia Croft
Proofreader: Cathy Peck
Step-by-Step Photography: Derek Fell
Garden Plans: Elayne Sears and Storey Communications, Inc.

All of us at Meredith® Books are dedicated to providing you with the information and ideas you need for successful gardening. We guarantee your satisfaction with this book for as long as you own it. If you have any questions, comments, or suggestions, please write to us at:

Meredith® Books, *Garden Books*
Editorial Department, RW206
1716 Locust St.
Des Moines, IA 50309–3023

Library of Congress Catalog Card Number: 94-74291
ISBN: 0-696-20655-2

STEP-BY-STEP

Wildflowers & Native Plants

The World of Wildflowers

*A*merica has always been partly wild, and its poets and philosophers have always loved the wilder part of nature. • "How fitting," wrote Henry David Thoreau, "to have every day in a vase of water on your table the wild-flowers of the season which are just blossoming! Can any house be said to be furnished without them? Shall we be so forward to pluck the fruits of Nature and neglect her flowers?" • Obviously if you are reading this book and are planning a garden of wildflowers, the answer to Thoreau's questions is no—and you have joined a great tradition.

Some Necessary Definitions

The following definitions are used by the National Wildflower Research Center.

Wildflowers: *Flowering plants native to a specific geographic area or habitat and capable of growing in unimproved habitats without the assistance of humans. Wildflowers often include naturalized species that coexist with other plants but are not aggressively competitive or invasive.*

Native plants: *Grasses, shrubs, vines, trees, and herbaceous wildflowers that exist in a given region without having been artificially introduced.*

Naturalized plants: *Plants that were introduced by humans but have escaped from cultivation.*

Why do wildflowers differ from blossoms found in typical North American gardens? And how did so many wildflowers from Europe and Asia end up growing in our own woods and fields?

Consider the word *wild*, which is defined as something that grows without human assistance, as a product of nature alone. And that's just what a wildflower is: a plant that has always been on its own without any human intervention. In fact, all the flowers in our gardens derive from wildflowers.

A distinction can be made between wildflowers in general and native plants. Native plants (including trees and shrubs as well as flowers) grow well on their own, without assistance from a gardener, in the area where they originated. Some plants are native to very specific places; the Venus's-flytrap *(Dionaea muscipula)*, for example, is found in a few sites in the Carolinas. Such region-specific plants can easily become endangered, or even extinct, if their limited natural habitat is destroyed through development or natural disaster or if too many plants are collected from the wild to be sold.

Although all native plants are wild, not all wildflowers are natives. Some of the plants we assume are native, such as the tawny daylily *(Hemerocallis fulva)* that is a familiar summer sight along roadsides in the eastern United States, actually originated elsewhere (the tawny daylily is native to Europe and Asia). Brought here many years ago, these plants eventually escaped from cultivation and began to grow and reproduce on their own.

▼ How Wildflowers Spread

Plants spread from one place to another in a number of ways. Seeds may be carried in the intestines of birds or other animals, or travel on people's shoes or in pants' cuffs, in livestock feed, or in shipments of other plants. Sometimes seeds are carried by strong winds or hurricanes.

Probably the largest number of plants accidentally introduced in this country arrived in ships' ballast. Because the early merchant ships that sailed from Europe were empty of goods on the trip over, their hulls were loaded with dirt so that they would float properly. When they arrived in the Americas, the dirt was removed and left onshore. The seeds it contained then began to sprout, bloom, produce more seed, and eventually spread.

Other plants, like the tawny daylily, set only sterile seed. Brought here intentionally by early settlers, they spread when a rhizome crept under a fence or when plants were tossed out of gardens with weed clippings. Today, winter plows or summer roadwork crews may chop up daylilies growing alongside country roads and scatter enough pieces of root for the plants to roam.

One of the few problems in growing wildflowers is identifying them by their common names. "Snakeroot" can mean one plant to southeastern gardeners and an entirely different plant to northeasterners. So it is best to use the scientific name when ordering plants. To simplify matters, today most nurseries list their plants with both common and scientific names.

▼ Planning a Wildflower Garden

There are many kinds of beautiful wildflowers. Two native American species, the large white wake-robin *(Trillium grandiflorum)* and the huge and magnificent Turk's-cap lily *(Lilium superbum)*, are so beautiful in bloom that they can outshine the best of the garden perennials. Other wildflowers, like the demure

Queen-Anne's-lace (Daucus carota *var.* carota) *is a biennial wildflower that originally came from Eurasia but has now naturalized throughout North America.*

one-flowered pyrola *(Moneses uniflora)* or the blue-flowered bluets *(Houstonia caerulea)*, are small with a delicate, quiet beauty that is often overlooked by eyes accustomed to today's bigger, flashier garden flowers. Still other wildflowers have a fleeting beauty, blooming for only a brief time and requiring special care when they are planted out, even in the wildflower garden. They include the lovely bloodroot *(Sanguinaria canadensis)*, whose petals fall within a week of the buds' opening, and the incredibly beautiful Virginia bluebells *(Mertensia virginica)*, which are covered with bright blue bells in early spring but completely disappear from the garden by the beginning of summer.

Some wildflowers that are attractive in fields or forests are not recommended for gardens, even gardens that are dedicated to native plants. Most members of the mint family, including the invasive but pretty ground ivy *(Glechoma hederacea)*, either have charming little flowers or provide wonderful aromatic fragrances, but they usually grow so aggressively that they soon overrun most of the other wildflowers in their vicinity. The feathery seeds of wild lettuce *(Lactuca canadensis)* may be of interest to the gardener, but this wildflower has only very small yellow flowers at the top of 9-foot-high stems that are lightly clasped with toothed leaves. Most members of the mustard family, including the yellow-flowered black mustard *(Brassica nigra)* found along roads, are pretty from a distance but look too wild for even the wildest corner of the garden.

The majority of wildflowers, however, have a special charm. The magic of gardening with these lovely plants comes not only from their alluring flowers but also from the way they attract an endless variety of wildlife to your backyard. Although wildflowers can be pollinated by the honeybee, which came to America in the 1600s, they are also pollinated by a diverse group of native insects, including butterflies, moths, bumblebees, mining bees, wasps, beetles, and even ants, as well as hummingbirds. By growing wildflowers, you will attract many more of these visitors to your backyard than you will with a garden devoted to typical annuals and perennials like petunias, marigolds, and irises. And wildflowers are usually tough—once established in the proper environment, they are very easy to care for.

Keep in mind that wildflower gardens call for an entirely different approach to design. Few are suited to the grand floral borders that we have inherited from the English garden tradition. The beauty of wildflowers is often lost when they are planted in masses. Instead, set them out in intimate designs that can be viewed close up, such as a small garden designed with an eye to seasonal blooming. These intimate layouts are well suited to the relatively small backyards of many of today's homes. Grand perennial borders may be effective on grand estates, but for most average American homes, wildflowers make the perfect garden complement.

▼ Wildflower Conservation

Unfortunately, a few wildflowers, often innocently brought from other habitats, have become major threats to native flora. An example of such an outlaw plant is purple loosestrife *(Lythrum salicaria)*, which was brought here from Europe on old sailing ships and has become the scourge of wetlands in the Northeast and upper Midwest. Although the loosestrife cultivars sold by nurseries are mostly self-sterile (meaning that they do not usually produce seeds by themselves, and must be propagated vegetatively) and

Plants can become endangered for a number of reasons, but often the cause is loss of habitat due to land development. In the case of an endangered coneflower, Echinacea tennesseensis, the plant's range is so small that interbreeding has caused the species to become genetically weak and unable to expand its range. These plants are being cultivated to preserve them.

The National Wildflower Research Center

The National Wildflower Research Center (NWRC) is an organization devoted to the study of wildflowers and native grasses, shrubs, and trees. It is committed to protecting and reestablishing native flora wherever possible. To that end the NWRC strongly encourages the propagation of native plants and their use in the landscape.

The NWRC also suggests the control of invasive species when needed and deplores the introduction of foreign species to native flora as unwise and unnecessary.

The NWRC believes that the reestablishment of native plant species will provide aesthetic beauty, help in the sound management of water and other resources, and support the ecological stability of different regions.

The address of the NWRC is 4801 La Crosse Boulevard, Austin, TX 78739. Phone (512) 292- 4100.

have traded many of their invasive qualities for enhanced color, the wild variety has not. *L. salicaria* has no enemies and cheerfully crowds out all native plants. Vast areas of New York, Pennsylvania, and New England—once dotted with wildflowers of all descriptions—are now stained purple with loosestrife plants blooming in late July and August. The problem is so bad that it is now illegal to grow wild varieties of purple loosestrife in several states.

Of greater concern, however, are the dangers that wildflowers face, not the damage that they do. Many native plants, especially those that exist in small habitats, are threatened by unbridled development as woodlands are cut for lumber and land is cleared for shopping malls and vacation homes. Most developers are more interested in clearing the land than in protecting native plants. Working with a local or national organization dedicated to preserving wildflowers, you may help to counter this trend by getting the property owner's permission to move plants that stand in the way of a bulldozer or backhoe.

Another threat is posed by unscrupulous nurseries that take plants from the wild. For example, so many Venus's-flytraps have been removed from their original swampy homes in eastern North Carolina that few now exist in the wild. If not for the development of tissue culture, this particular species might have disappeared forever.

To discourage such plundering of wildflowers, buy propagated plants only from honest and reliable nurseries. Never patronize a truck that appears at a farmer's market loaded with pots of wildflowers.

Wild orchids are especially popular at such sales, but few will last in the home garden because they lack the necessary fungal associations to guarantee their survival. And when you see blooming trilliums priced at an astounding three dollars each, think about the eventual cost of such a bargain. The artificially low price of these inferior plants will end up costing you more money when you must replace them after they die in the garden. For information on good sources of wildflowers, check the resources section on pages 128–129.

To learn more about protecting and growing wildflowers, become active in one or more of the many preservation groups devoted to the protection of native plants. Some, like the National Wildflower Research Center based in Austin, Texas, or the Canadian Wildflower Society in Ontario, are devoted to the entire North American continent. Others, such as the New England Wild Flower Society in Framingham, Massachusetts, specialize in regional aspects of growing wildflowers. There are also dozens of organizations dedicated to only one wildflower genus and various native plant societies that specialize in regional wildflower habitats. Finally, a number of plant societies feature seed exchanges. To find the names and addresses of plant societies that may interest you, see the sidebar on page 49 or consult the excellent sourcebook *Gardening by Mail* by Barbara J. Barton (see page 128).

California poppies (Esch-scholzia californica) are annuals or short-lived perennials, depending on the climate in which they grow. In either case these poppies are among the most beautiful of wildflowers.

A restored prairie in Texas glows with native wildflowers and grasses, offering a combination of beauty and informality.

CHAPTER 1

Designing Wildflower Gardens

*M*ost wildflowers are beautiful plants that have adapted themselves over time—without the gardener's aid—to particular environments. Outside these environments, unlike most popular garden perennials, they simply fold up and die if their special requirements are ignored. • But if properly treated—and sited—most wildflowers will quickly adapt to a garden setting. Then, over the years, they will fend for themselves, making far fewer demands than their more cultivated cousins. • The first step to creating a wildflower garden is the garden's design. This chapter will show you, step by step, how to design a beautiful and successful wildflower garden.

Wildflower Environments

Grasses for Prairie Gardens

Big bluestem (Andropogon gerardii) *grows 4 to 10 feet tall, and little bluestem* (Schizachyrium scoparium) *reaches a height of 2 to 5 feet. Blue grama* (Bouteloua gracilis), *native to the High Plains, grows in a low bunch about 1½ feet tall when in flower. Sweetgrass, or basket grass* (Hierochloe odorata), *about 3 feet tall, smells of vanilla and has long been used in making baskets. Switch-grass* (Panicum virgatum), *4 to 10 feet tall, has beautiful seed heads and blades that turn orange-yellow in winter. Indian grass* (Sorghastrum avenaceum), *2 to 5 feet tall, forms plumelike seed heads in September. Prairie cord-grass* (Spartina pectinata) *produces 2½-foot blades that wave and fold like fanciful ribbons.*

*T*o be successful, a wildflower garden should provide growing conditions that are similar to those in the plants' natural habitat. Before designing a wildflower garden, therefore, you need to understand the different types of environments in which native plants are found in the wild. Most plants have definite climate preferences. Some like it hot; some like it cold. Some want dry soil; others need a bit of damp or even outright wetness at the roots. In countries as large as the United States and Canada, the number of native plants reaches into the thousands—yet few, if any, species are ubiquitous. Our wildflowers and native plants are found in certain prescribed environments that nature has tailored for them. These different growing conditions are described below.

▼ Dry, Wet, and Alpine Meadows

Dry meadows are treeless plains dominated by grasses and interspersed with spring-, summer-, and fall-blooming perennials and some annuals. Today meadows are on the increase across much of America because in many places farmland is being abandoned. Fields once planted for hay production become host to additional grasses and wildflowers when annual cuttings stop, and within a short time bushes and scrub trees take root. Before larger and more permanent trees take hold, however, the open meadow boasts grasses that wave in summer breezes and wildflowers that dot the green with spots of color. Examples of meadow grasses are little bluestem *(Schizachyrium scoparium)*, switch-grass *(Panicum virgatum)*, and Indian grass *(Sorghastrum avenaceum)*. Flowers include goldenrods *(Solidago* spp.*)*, asters *(Aster* spp.*)*, beebalm *(Monarda didyma)*, and purple coneflower *(Echinacea purpurea)*.

Wet meadows are low-lying treeless areas in full sun where there is always water in the soil. They are not to be confused with fresh meadows, where water is found in late winter to early spring but usually dries up in summer heat. Many wildflowers flourish in wet conditions, including great blue lobelia *(Lobelia siphilitica)* and cardinal flower *(L. cardinalis)*.

An alpine meadow is high ground consisting of poor but well-drained soil with lots of gravel, shards, and other small stones. Here the grasses are low to the ground and the wildflowers consist of species such as alpine bellflowers *(Campanula* spp.*)*, various thymes *(Thymus* spp.*)*, and pinks *(Dianthus* spp.*)*.

▼ Prairies

Prairies are the treeless midwestern grasslands where great herds of buffalo once roamed. They are categorized as tallgrass or shortgrass prairies—or combinations of both—according to the amount of rainfall they receive, which determines how high the grasses grow. Within these prairies are dozens of grass species that fall into two broad categories: warm-season and cool-season grasses.

During the summer, warm-season grasses stay green and grow actively; they become dormant when temperatures are cool, and their green color changes to tan and brown. These grasses are very drought resistant. Cool-season grasses begin to grow early in the spring and stay green long into the fall but are dormant during the hot months of summer, unless they are given lots of water.

There's more to prairies than grasses: Their wildflowers are legion. Among the most beautiful species

1 *The key to success with wildflowers is providing a garden environment like the plant's natural habitat. These asters are growing wild in a dry meadow.*

2 *Asters from the garden center will thrive in a meadow garden. Plant at the same depth the plants were growing in their pots, and retain as much of the soil ball as possible.*

Outstanding Plants for Deciduous Woodlands
Good plants for woodland shade include goatsbeard (Aruncus dioicus), 6-foot plants with compound leaves and showy plumes of tiny white flowers; fairy-candles (Cimicifuga americana), which have good foliage and slender wands of tiny white flowers up to 4 feet tall; bunchberry (Cornus canadensis), with creamy white petals (really bracts) followed by red berries; and white snakeroot (Eupatorium rugosum), with white powder-puff flowers on top of 3-foot stems. Bowman's-root (Gillenia trifoliata) has thin-petaled white or pink flowers that flutter on 3-foot stems. The beautiful white wake-robin (Trillium grandiflorum) bears showy three-petaled flowers that turn deep pink with age on 14-inch stems.

are Culver's root *(Veronicastrum virginicum)*; thick-spike gay-feather or prairie blazing star *(Liatris pycnostachya)*; the unusual-looking rattlesnake-master *(Eryngium yuccifolium)*, spiderwort *(Tradescantia* spp.*)*, New England aster *(Aster novae-angliae)*, and oxeye *(Heliopsis helianthoides)*.

▼ Woodlands

Not all North American forests are alike. In the vast coniferous forests full of evergreens, the floors are thick with needles from previous years and ferns surround the tree trunks like a textured lawn. In the temperate rain forests of the Northwest, giant sequoias have grown for thousands of years.

Probably the best-known American forests, however, are the fabled woodlands in the temperate Northeast, which once spread from the Atlantic westward to the prairies. Here the overhead canopy of coniferous and deciduous trees allows full sun to reach the forest floor during the winter but permits only filtered sun during the hottest (and often driest) part of the year. Wildflowers and ferns (see page 17) abound in these woodlands.

▼ Bogs and Swamps

Bogs and swamps are both continually wet, but the bottom of a bog consists of accumulations of peat instead of the mud and decayed vegetation found in a swamp. Plants that can tolerate the wet conditions in both environments include marsh marigold *(Caltha palustris)* and rose mallow *(Hibiscus palustris)*.

Even if you do not have wet conditions on your property, it is relatively easy to construct a small bog

Wildflower Environments CONTINUED

Carnivorous Plants for Bogs

Bizarre yet beautiful insect-eating plants are right at home in bog gardens. Venus's-flytrap (Dionaea muscipula), zones 8 to 9 south, has spine-edged, hinged leaves that close on a small fly or bug, then slowly digest it; its spring flowers are small, white, and delicate. In zones 5 to 8 the cobra lily (Darlingtonia californica) produces 3-foot tubes with hooded tops. The common pitcher plant (Sarracenia purpurea) produces red-veined basal leaves that are swollen in the center and covered by a two-lobed lid that holds water and attracts insects. The flower of the pitcher plant resembles an umbrella, with reddish sepals and red petals growing upside down. These plants will grow—but produce fewer flowers—without their insect food.

The cobra lily (Darlingtonia californica) was discovered in 1841 in a marsh near the Sacramento River. The plant is only hardy to zone 8, but it can be grown in a terrarium.

Marsh marigolds love moist, boggy places and even grow directly in water. This white species (Caltha leptosepala) is found in the western part of the United States.

In this leafy glade, creeping phlox (P. stolonifera) *combines beautifully with Christmas fern* (Polystichum acrostichoides) *and ostrich fern* (Matteuccia struthiopteris).

garden for wildflowers. Dig a hole in the soil and bury an old bathtub to its rim, then cover that edge with flat stones. Or make a large shallow bowl that will hold wet earth by digging a hole, installing a plastic pool or pond liner (available from water-garden supply companies), then covering the liner with 1½ to 2 feet of soil. Water as often as necessary to keep the soil wet. (See page 67.)

▼ Streamsides and Ponds

With plenty of water, you can grow plants that root in wet soil or prefer to grow in water. Your options include digging a pond and then lining it with clay or making a small pond using one of the new plastic or rubber pond liners. Grow turtleheads *(Chelone glabra)* and boneset *(Eupatorium perfoliatum)* at the water's edge, and let water lilies *(Nymphaea spp.)* and spatterdocks *(Nuphar advena)* share space in the pond with arrowheads *(Sagittaria latifolia)* and cat-tails *(Typha latifolia).* (For more examples of plants to grow in pools and ponds, see page 18.)

If you're lucky enough to have a moving stream on your property, there are wonderful wildflowers to plant along the water's edge. Joe-Pye weed *(Eupatorium purpureum)* can reach 10 feet, and its clusters of tiny pink-purple flowers are magnets for butterflies. Yellow flag *(Iris pseudacorus)* produces sword-shaped leaves and lovely yellow flowers.

▼ The Desert

Deserts may not be just sand but may include vast expanses of rock and gravel. They are distinguished by a lack of water and, when water does appear, by rapid drainage. Amazingly, many of the wildflowers in true deserts can wait—sometimes for years—for rain to fall. Then they seem to bloom overnight. A

Wildflower Environments CONTINUED

Water Plants for Pools and Ponds

The leaves of the sweet flag (Acorus americanus) *or the flowers and bladelike leaves of the water iris make them wonderful plants for a fresh-water pond. Both common arrowhead* (Sagittaria latifo-lia) *and pickerel weed* (Pontederia cordata) *have attractive leaves and lovely flowers. In small ponds wild rice* (Zizania aquatica) *can either be planted in sub-merged pots or sown directly in the water. Other water plants, such as cattails* (Typha spp.), *horsetails* (Equisetum spp.), *and most of the sedges and rushes* (Juncus spp.), *also do well in that environment. Plant cat-tails and horsetails in pots, or they will take over.*

1 *The spring-blooming Texas bluebonnet* (Lupinus texen-sis) *is an annual wildflower that serves as an indicator plant for alkaline soil conditions.*

2 *The Eastern trout lily, or amberbell* (Erythronium ameri-canum), *is a perennial wildflower that prefers an acid soil rich in woodland humus.*

3 *The prickly pear, or barbary fig cactus* (Opuntia vulgar-is), *is a perennial that grows well in dry, sandy soil or well-drained, rocky soil.*

4 *Native cattails* (Typha spp.) *and purple loosestrife* (Lythrum salicaria), *naturalized aliens outlawed in many states, are both indicator plants for wet and boggy soil.*

An alpine garden provides the excellent drainage needed by most mountain wildflowers.

Plants for Scree Beds

*Scree beds filled with crushed rocks and soil provide perfect drainage and are best for plants that resent any standing moisture at their roots. Among the plants that will do well in garden soil or in a scree are columbines, especially the common wild columbine (*Aquilegia canadensis) *and the Colorado columbine (A. caerulea). Other plants include hairy golden aster (*Chrysopsis villosa), *giant wild rye (*Elymus condensatus), *many of the goldenrods (*Solidago spp.), *desert marigold (*Baileya multiradiata), *desert dandelion (*Malacothrix glabrata), *squirreltail grass (*Hordeum jubatum), *desert lily (*Hesperocallis undulata), *most of the needlegrasses (*Stipa spp.), *and yuccas (*Yucca spp.).*

backyard desert can contain many wildflowers, including prickly pear cactus *(Opuntia* spp.*)*, desert marigold *(Baileya multiradiata)*, desert zinnia *(Z. grandiflora)*, and goldenrod *(Solidago* spp.*)*.

▼ Screes and Rocky Slopes

Screes and rocky slopes are the domain of the rock gardener. In both these environments the soil consists of rock shards and small bits of gravel along with some sand. Plants needing perfect drainage and poor soil, such as the Colorado columbine *(Aquilegia caerulea)*, grow beautifully. You can create a scree bed for alpine plants in your garden if your soil is not naturally rocky (see the sidebar on this page and on page 25).

▼ Pine Barrens

The pine barrens found near coastal areas have shallow sandy soil of high acidity and low fertility. As their name implies, they are full of pines. Other vegetation usually includes hollies, low-growing shrubs, and often poison ivy and poison oak. They are also home to prickly pears, sandworts *(Minuartia caroliniana,* formerly *Arenaria caroliniana)*, and sand myrtles *(Leiophyllum buxifolium)*.

▼ Seashore and Sand Dunes

When visiting an inland sand dune or the shores of the ocean, you'll see that the landscape is not barren. Grasses, succulent plants, low bushes, goldenrods, and even wild roses can adapt to the wind and, near

Wildflower Environments CONTINUED

Even the harsh environment of the seashore will support hundreds of wildflower species. Here, along the Pacific Coast, plants have adapted to strong sun, high winds, salt spray, and sandy or rock-laced soil.

the ocean, to salt spray. But be warned: Both poison ivy and poison oak also root with ease.

Just remember that sandy soil quickly loses water. If this is the sort of environment in which you will plant, pass up perennials that suffer when water rations are short and instead use wild plants that can send their roots deep into the earth and survive until the next rainfall. Northern sea oats *(Chasmanthium latifolium)*, American beach grass *(Ammophila breviligulata)*, many species of native roses *(Rosa* spp.*)*, blue false indigo *(Baptisia australis)*, beebalm *(Monarda didyma)*, tawny daylily *(Hemerocallis fulva)*,

Turk's-cap lily *(Lilium superbum)*, and the many goldenrods *(Solidago* spp.*)* will do well in a seashore environment. You should also be able to grow some native annuals, including California poppy *(Eschscholzia californica)*, flowering tobacco *(Nicotiana* spp.*)*, coreopsis *(C. tinctoria)*, and larkspur *(Consolida ambigua)*.

This desert garden supports jumping cholla (Opuntia fulgida), a large cactus species that bears lovely pink flowers in spring. There is also a mix of desert wild-flowers.

Another name for the marsh marigold is cowslip. Here is Caltha palustris 'Flore Plena', a cultivar of great charm that boasts double flowers.

Assessing Your Site

When creating new beds and borders, use a garden hose to lay out curves and edgings before you start to dig. And if you are using bricks for an edging, make sure the curves are large enough to absorb the straight lines of the individual bricks.

A wildflower garden should look natural, as if the plants had always been in that spot. Don't just carve a geometric island bed out of a lawn and fill it with wildflowers. Wildflowers look and grow best in a garden that resembles their native habitat.

The first step to a well-designed and flourishing wildflower garden is understanding the natural elements of the part of the world you live in, beginning with the general climate. Once you know the high and low temperatures of your region, walk around your property, taking note of its positive features as well as its limitations. Examine the general lay of the land, the type of soil, individual landmarks, possible microclimates, and windbreaks. Lastly, consider your own inclinations, especially your gardening likes and dislikes.

If you don't already know the climate zone you live in, consult the map on page 127 or call your county cooperative extension office. If you live in upstate Maine, don't try to grow wildflowers that bloom south of the Mason-Dixon Line. In New Orleans, it's impossible (unless you install refrigeration equipment) to grow bunchberries *(Cornus canadensis)*.

If you live in a part of the country where rainfall is slight, especially in spring and during the height of summer, you should choose wildflowers that stand up to dry conditions—there are hundreds of plants that prefer these growing conditions. On the other hand, wet areas demand plants that do not object to excess water in the soil; again, there are hundreds of plants that fit the bill.

How much sun you get is another factor to consider. Many wildflowers bloom when spring first arrives, before the trees overhead begin to leaf out. But they continue to grow long after the trees shade their locale. Others must have full sun to grow and flower. Make a small map of your property showing the varying amounts of sun and shade in different areas.

If strong winds are frequent, you must find a protected spot for the new garden or create a windbreak. Remember the windchill factor. A temperature of 0°F feels like −44°F when a 25 mph wind is blowing, and plants feel windchill just as people do.

Check if there are any natural features that will work to your advantage. It's amazing how many lots are blessed with a natural grove of trees, a stream, or a large, attractive boulder. Whether you have an older home or are building from scratch on your own land, look for something that could become a garden feature. Also keep an eye out for a small dip or gully that would provide extra winter protection in a cold climate or relief from summer sun in the South. Or if there's a wet area, think about creating a small pool (see photos on page 24).

Determine what kind of soil you have. If your soil is pure clay, adding organic matter will help it drain better while still holding moisture. Looser soil will expand your plant choices. Organic matter also improves sandy soil. So start a compost heap and gather leaves to shred and then add to the soil. Begin by improving one area, then go on to another. Test the pH, the acidity or alkalinity, of your soil as well (see the sidebar on page 60 for more about pH). Many wildflowers have a decided preference for acid, neutral, or alkaline soil. Contact your county cooperative extension office and find out how to have your soil tested or buy a good-quality pH test kit at the garden center.

1 *Clay soil is sticky when wet and forms large, hard lumps when dry. It contains many minerals and trace elements.*

2 *Sandy soil is fine and porous, containing few nutrients. Water passes through this type of soil with ease.*

3 *Humus, sometimes called black earth, is the result of decaying vegetable matter in the soil. It is very fertile.*

4 *Loam is soil that is neither too light nor too heavy; il is usually rich in organic matter and reasonably fertile.*

Assessing Your Site CONTINUED

▼ **Assessing the Climate**

When a weather forecaster reports freezing temperatures in your area, don't believe every word. In most places, conditions vary somewhat across a geographic region due to various local factors. For example, if you live in a valley protected from bitter winds, your garden may be warmer than that of your friend who lives on top of a hill. If you have a small city garden surrounded by buildings and roadways, the temperature in your backyard will be warmer than in gardens out in the country. Gardens at high elevations are colder than gardens closer to sea level. And large bodies of water have a moderating effect on the climate in their vicinity.

Local variations in weather conditions are known as microclimates, and they can have a profound effect on the garden. As you assess your site in preparation for designing a wildflower garden (or any other kind of garden), pay attention to microclimates on your property. You may find exposed spots where plants need protection to survive in winter or sheltered locations where plants that are usually not hardy in your area will thrive.

Plants native to your locality are a good place to start planning a wildflower garden because they thrive in climatic conditions like those in your garden. From native plants you can branch out to include plants native to other places where the climate and growing conditions are similar to those in your area. Ask your county cooperative extension office or a local botanical garden for a list of the native trees and plants found in your area of the country.

1 *If you have a self-contained stream on your property, create a small pool by bringing large, flat stones to the site and laying them across the streambed.*

2 *Try planting sweet flag (*Acorus americanus*) or marsh marigold (*Caltha palustris*) next to your new pool. These wildflowers love wet areas.*

Planning a Garden

Creating a Scree Bed

If your soil is poor, you can make a scree bed for alpine plants by constructing a low rock wall up to 2½ feet high. Fill the bed behind the wall with a mix of two parts pea gravel and one part each of shredded compost and good garden soil. The resulting fill will have perfect drainage yet provide more than adequate nutrition for plants.

*F*or any garden project, start by taking paper and pencil and sketching a simple map of the area to be developed and planted. Your drawing does not need to be complicated, but sketching your property will help you to focus on what is possible.

Only you can decide how much of a garden you wish to care for and how much time and money you have to spend. Tending to a garden always takes more time than you think, and it can be depressing to look at an abandoned site where a few struggling plants are being overwhelmed by weeds because you bit off more than you could chew. If you are new to gardening, start small; you can always expand the garden next year.

On your map indicate the presence of natural windbreaks, existing trees, the direction of the worst winter winds, possible obstructions to spring and fall sunlight, and all structures—whether already in place or planned for the future. As you plan, remember that the key word for growing wildflowers is *natural*.

If you want a woodland garden and the developer left your new house surrounded by dirt and sparse grass, start planting trees immediately. Select fast-growing trees suited to your area (ask a reputable local nursery or your county cooperative extension agent for suggestions). You do not need a forest to grow woodland wildflowers—only some shade. Even a ring of fast-growing shrubs will suffice. When planted in a triangle, three trees will quickly make a miniature woodland with several different kinds of shade. The south side will have sun most of the day, the north will be in deep shade all day, the east will get morning sun, and the west will have afternoon sun.

If your house is already in a wooded area with lots of shade, you probably yearn for a sunny wildflower garden but can't afford or don't wish to cut a number

Use a scree bed for plants needing perfect drainage. Here a native, Sedum nevii, grows in a scree of stones, crushed rock, and cow manure.

of trees in order to open up the landscape. You could instead try some selective pruning. Remove lower tree limbs to open up more light and air, and clean out any choking underbrush.

▼ Work with Your Land

If there is a poorly drained spot on your land, instead of fussing about drainage, turn the area into a bog garden. If there is a drainage ditch that is rarely wet, fill it with crushed stones and create a desert garden. If you have one big and glorious tree, remove the grass underneath it and plant ferns and shade-loving wildflowers instead. If there is a large open area with a lot of sun, you could plant a meadow or put in a small pond where water lilies can bloom in the sun and dragonflies flit from lily pad to lily pad. If you have a low spot with terrible drainage, build a low

Planning a Garden CONTINUED

stone wall and make a raised-bed wildflower garden. If you have too much existing lawn, turn some into a meadow or prairie garden.

▼ Start with Tough Plants

At first choose the toughest and most adaptable plants for the environment you have. Queen-Anne's-lace, purple coneflower, and black-eyed Susan are good choices. As you begin to learn about wildflower behaviors and growing patterns, you can think about growing the rarer and more difficult plants.

▼ Plan Ahead

Think of how your garden will look throughout the year. Virginia bluebells (*Mertensia virginica*), for example, are lovely in the spring, but they disappear by the time summer rolls around. Their roots are still present beneath the soil, but nothing of the plants shows aboveground. In such a case, plant two wild-flowers, one for the spring and one for the rest of the growing season.

Also remember to think about fall color. Bluestar (*Amsonia tabernaemontana*), for example, is especially beautiful when autumn arrives. And some plants have interesting seedpods. The plumelike seed heads of the pasqueflower (*Anemone patens*), sometimes called prairie smoke, are as beautiful as the flower that produced them. For more on planning for seasonal interest, see pages 28–29.

Also consider a plant's mature height when planning the garden. Unless you are trying for a special effect, put tall plants at the rear and short plants in the front of your garden.

▼ Look at Other Gardens

There's nothing wrong with looking at other gardeners' solutions to a problem and then adapting their ideas to your own backyard. You can also visit wildflower gardens in your area, and check if a local botanical garden or arboretum has an area reserved for wildflower displays.

TROUBLESHOOTING TIP

When choosing wildflowers for use in the landscape, be sure to consider the foliage as well as the blooms. Wildflower leaves come in a variety of shapes, colors, and textures. By playing one against the other, the garden will be interesting even when not in bloom. Remember, too, that variegated plants are especially attractive in a shady or wooded setting.

Plant summer bloomers, such as butterfly weed (Asclepias tuberosa) *shown here, along with spring-blooming wildflowers, such as Virginia bluebells* (Mertensia virginica). *When the pale blue flowers of the bluebells die back in summer, the bright orange flowers of butterfly weed will fill out any gaps in the garden.*

In this simple garden design, common columbines (Aquilegia canadensis) grow with hay-scented ferns (Dennstaedtia punctilobula).

Early Bloomers

One of the first flowers of spring is the Tussilago far-fara, *a European flower commonly called coltsfoot that has naturalized in America. In the Catskill Mountains of New York, it will often bloom in mid- to late February, depending on the winter. It can be invasive, however. A more genteel flower for early spring is the spring-beauty* (Claytonia vir-ginica), *with its loose clusters of small, fragrant, pink flowers with deep pink veins. Another is bloodroot* (Sanguinaria canadensis), *which blooms with fairly large white starry flowers on 8-inch stems.*

Seasonal Interest

Wildflowers that Produce Berries

Many wildflowers follow their blooms with colorful berries. False Solomon's-seal (Smilacina racemosa) produces showy red, speckled berries that persist into winter. The yellow-flowered bluebead lily (Clintonia borealis) bears lovely blue berries in a cool, moist spot with very acid soil. The red fall berries of the jack-in-the-pulpit (Arisaema triphyllum) are bright and beautiful. The bright red berries of partridgeberry (Mitchella repens) are so long-lasting they are often used in terrariums or Christmas decorations. The clusters of red berries on the bunchberry (Cornus canadensis) can light up the woodland on a rainy autumn afternoon. Bearberry (Arctostaphylos uva-ursi) is a great ground cover for sunny, dry slopes in well-drained soil and has bright red berries in fall.

*U*nless your garden is in a tropical rain forest, you will have summer, winter, spring, and fall. In some areas, autumn brings the beginning of the rainy season instead of brilliant color in the trees. And gardeners in the Far North may be more interested in the winter garden, when colorful berries and attractive seedpods are of prime importance, because the frost-free growing season in their region is all too brief. But no matter where you live or which season is your favorite, you should think about seasonal interest. Try to plan your garden to have something blooming most of the growing year, from early spring to late fall, or year-round in warm climates.

Choose wildflowers that not only have pretty flowers but also produce attractive seed heads or berries. The seedpods of blue false indigo *(Baptisia australis)* are fascinating both in the garden and in a vase. Pearly everlasting *(Anaphalis margaritacea)* has flowers that are pretty in bloom and also dry beautifully. These flowers, which resemble strawflowers, are true to their name, seeming almost everlasting on plants in the garden and really lasting forever when dried and brought indoors for winter bouquets. The seedpods of the butterfly weed *(Asclepias tuberosa)* soon betray its relation to the large milkweeds of the field. But they are lovely when they open and the silky seeds fly out upon the winds of late summer and early fall.

When cold weather appears on the scene, you need not ignore the wildflower garden, especially if you have included plants that catch the eye in winter. Colorful berries, intriguing seedpods, and evergreen leaves all add interest to the garden when the snow falls. Especially popular are the red berries of bunchberry *(Cornus canadensis)* and the orange-red berries of jack-in-the-pulpit *(Arisaema triphyllum)*. The crimson berries of false Solomon's-seal *(Smilacina*

Wintergreen, or teaberry (Gaultheria procumbens), *is a marvelous evergreen ground cover that bears nodding white flowers followed by bright red berries that last into winter.*

racemosa) often persist into winter or at least until the birds eat them all. The evergreen leaves and red berries of the partridgeberry *(Mitchella repens)* decorate the forest floor through a light dusting of snow, and they will do the same in your garden. As a bonus for wildlife-watchers, birds love feasting on the berries. Wintergreen *(Gaultheria procumbens)*, which also has evergreen leaves and red berries, offers a similar effect (see the above photo). The evergreen leaves of coltsfoot *(Galax urceolata)* are bronzed around the edges in fall and winter but still retain their lovely glistening surface, even when coated with ice. The leaves of the tiny trailing arbutus *(Epigaea repens)* are evergreen. This plant is rare, so when buying it be sure you are getting a nursery-propagated plant, not one collected from the wild.

Bunchberry (Cornus canadensis) *is a small ground-hugging relative of the dogwood tree. The white flowers of spring are followed by bright red fruits in the fall.*

The dried flowers and seed heads of other plants are another source of interest in winter gardens. The tall brown spires of mulleins *(Verbascum thapsus, V. blattaria,* and *V. phoeniceum)* are stately, sometimes reaching a height of 7 or 8 feet. The dried and opened seedpods of the yuccas *(Yucca* spp.*)* are also handsome, adding a sculptural touch to the garden as they stand sentry above their sword-shaped evergreen leaves. The browned seed heads of gay-feather *(Liatris* spp.*)*, the brown baskets that are the dried flowers of Queen-Anne's-lace *(Daucus carota* var. *carota)*, and the dried flowers of goldenrods *(Solidago* spp.*)* are also attractive in the garden, especially when dusted with snow.

In the backyard or in open fields, the dried brown seed heads of yarrow *(Achillea millefolium)* will persist well into winter if you haven't cut the flowers to use in bouquets. The 4- to 6-foot stalks of American bugbane *(Cimicifuga americana)* and black cohosh *(C. racemosa)* retain their seedpods and look great in the garden when surrounded by snow. The prickly sharp seed heads of the common teasel *(Dipsacus* spp.*)* persist throughout the entire winter.

Finally, when planning for late-season interest, don't overlook the evergreen leaves of many American ferns, including the Christmas fern *(Polystichum acrostichoides)* and the maidenhair spleenwort *(Asplenium trichomanes)*. Grow the sensitive fern *(Onoclea sensibilis)* in order to enjoy its lovely spore cases, which look beautiful in winter in the garden or in dried arrangements.

Planning Pathways

When planning a wildflower garden, include some way to get to it, both to see the plants and for routine maintenance. To make the path fit in with your garden, choose materials that have a natural, rustic look, such as wood chips, gravel, log sections, stepping-stones, moss, cut or worn grass, beaten dirt, landscape ties, and pebbles or gravel.

The first thing to remember when making a pathway is that it must be sturdy enough to stand up to regular use. Next, it must be wide enough to allow the gardener to pass with a wheelbarrow or a small garden cart. And always try to curve it, even in a small garden: A straight path is boring. You can use a garden hose to experiment with different curves.

If your path traverses uneven terrain, you may want to install a few steps. Make them as wide as the path and no more than 5 or 6 inches high. Use stone curbing, split logs, long stones, or railroad ties, held with concrete reinforcement rods.

Finally, match the pathway and the materials used to the setting. Paths made of bark mulch, moss, or beaten dirt are perfect for a woodland garden but look out of place in the desert. Here are some suggestions for paths in different kinds of gardens.

▼ *Desert gardens:* Make a fake river of small stones, then set larger flat stones among or on top of them to walk on.

▼ *Meadow gardens:* Instead of making a permanent path, use a sickle bar or mower to cut 2½-foot channels through the tall grass (see page 85). Once cut, the grassy paths are easily maintained with a lawn

1 Tree branches make an appropriate border for a woodland path. With a chainsaw, cut branch sections to their proper length.

2 Make the path curve around a garden bed by using tree branches cut in short sections. Butt the ends of the sections together.

3 Narrow the path as it enters the woods to create an illusion of distance. When the last branch is in place, fill in the path with mulch.

1 A stepping-stone pathway can easily cross a small stream. Move stones to the site with a wheelbarrow.

2 Place a flat brace stone on each side of the stream to eventually hold the bridge stone.

3 Add more pathway stones on each side of the stream at a comfortable stepping distance. Finally, set the bridge stone in place.

4 When the pathway is completed, test the bridge stone to make sure it is securely placed above the stream and will hold your weight.

**E A R T H • W I S E
T I P**

To create interest when building a pathway, pay attention to the interplay of the path's materials with the textures of the garden. In a dry wild garden, try a river-like path of crushed stones with larger stepping-stones within its boundaries. A very effective pathway through a wildflower garden can be made of railroad ties set with the top surface at ground level.

Planning Pathways

The pathway of this West Coast garden passes through California poppies (Esch-scholzia californica) *and clarkias* (Clarkia unguicula-ta), *both native to California, along with borage* (Borago officinalis) *and flowering flax* (Linum grandiflorum).

1 *To cross a swampy area, build a raised board-walk or a simple log bridge. First inspect the site to determine placement.*

2 *Long side logs will brace the crosspieces and hold them in place. Lay these logs to cross the wet area.*

3 *Next, lay the shorter logs in place, side by side. Fasten them to the bracing logs with long waterproof nails.*

mower. In shortgrass meadows, use stepping-stones made of fieldstone or paths of loose gravel.

▼ *Bogs:* Plan on a path in which to place stepping-stones as you lay out the garden, or build a narrow boardwalk to cross the wet soil (this is the only case where a straight line should be used for a path).

▼ *Woodlands:* More path options exist for woodlands than for other gardens. For a permanent pathway, first plan the outlines with stakes and string, then remove any sod or surface growth. To prevent future weeds, use a commercial weed killer where the path will go or place a layer of plastic sheeting over the bare earth. Add a thin layer of sand for drainage, wet it, then tamp it with a commercial or homemade tamper. Now space stepping-stones along the pathway at a normal walking stride. Finish off the edges with flexible vinyl edging, and fill in the spaces around the stones with pea gravel, bark mulch, pine needles, or another natural material.

You can also use railroad ties as narrow stepping-stones. Cut them to the width of the path, then bury them so that they're just slightly above the surface of the ground. Or, if you have a large tree trunk, you can cut circles of wood about 2 or 3 inches thick, and sink them directly in the turf.

Another way to make a good woodland walk is to mulch the path and add new mulch whenever the covering grows thin. Or, if you don't anticipate a lot of foot traffic, simply pull out the grass, tamp down the remaining dirt, and wait for mosses to grow.

▼ *Seaside gardens:* Make a path of crushed oyster, clam, or other shells, or use pebbles or gravel from local sources.

A Meadow Garden

Before planting this garden for the first time, you need to prepare the soil. Turn over the ground, removing large stones and breaking up any big clods of dirt or roots. This is a good time to assess your soil. If your soil is sandy, it will dry quickly and species that do well in drier climates will thrive. If it is clay, it might drain poorly, so you should consider planting species that do well under moist conditions.

What could be more appropriate for native plants than a wildflower meadow, especially one that provides a colorful transition from a lawn to a natural area? This floral border is well positioned against a rustic fence that separates the more manicured part of the property from a neighboring field.

Wildflowers naturally lend themselves to an informal planting scheme like this one, which mimics a rural meadow. At the edge of the property, plant native species that are suited to the amount of sunlight the area receives. Once established, they will require very little attention other than occasional weeding. Choose a variety of plants so that you can have blooms from spring until fall, as different species come into their flowering season.

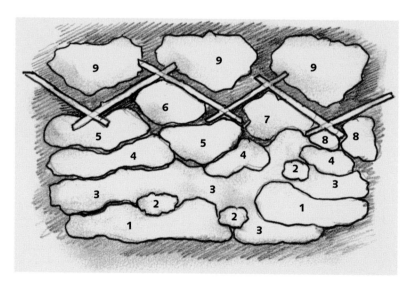

Plant List

1 Farewell-to-spring
(Clarkia amoena)
2 California poppy
(Eschscholzia californica)
3 Meadow foam
(Limnanthes douglasii)
4 Thick-spike gay-feather
(Liatris pycnostachya)
5 Lance-leaved coreopsis
(Coreopsis lanceolata)
6 Winecup
(Callirhoe involucrata)
7 Obedient plant
(Physostegia virginiana)
8 Purple coneflower
(Echinacea purpurea)
9 Queen-of-the-prairie
(Filipendula rubra)

After the flowering season is over, probably in late fall, wildflower meadows should be mowed to keep the woody and weedy plants from taking over. Since many native plants are annuals, some reseeding may be required from year to year in order to keep this garden going.

A Natural Desert Garden

As freshwater sources are becoming scarcer and more expensive, a gardening approach called Xeriscaping is gaining in popularity. The term is derived from the Greek word xeros, meaning "dry," and is applied to techniques that reduce the water required to maintain gardens. Xeriscaping stresses the establishment of landscapes adapted to the arid environments around them, rather than relying on moisture-loving species.

Where water is scarce, native plants provide a perfect landscaping solution, since they are adapted to the low precipitation levels. And because you won't need to water, you will have the added benefit of a garden that is truly low in maintenance.

Cacti and succulents come in an astonishing array of sizes, colors, and shapes, and many of them provide spectacular color when in bloom. Desert gardens, however, are not limited to cacti. There are hundreds of desert wildflowers, including many species of poppy, marigold, and verbena (as in the garden shown here), as well as penstemon, primrose, mallow, fairy duster, lupine, buckwheat, bluebell, and milkweed. With the desert's long growing season, an arid wildflower garden can be filled with color year-round.

Plant List
1 Pacific sedum
(Sedum spathulifolium)
2 Prickly pear
(Opuntia humifusa)
3 California bluebell
(Phacelia campanularia)
4 Matilija poppy
(Romneya coulteri)
5 Bush monkey flower
(Mimulus aurantiacus)
6 Adam's-needle
(Yucca filamentosa)
7 Desert marigold
(Baileya multiradiata)
8 Desert sand verbena
(Abronia villosa)

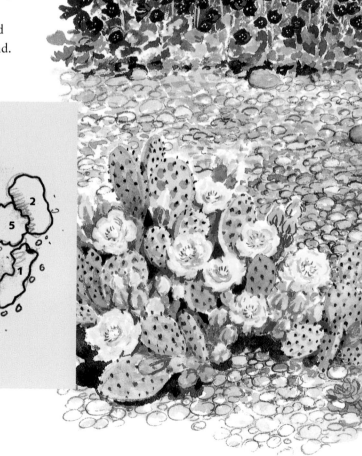

Using stones or gravel as ground cover can help the underlying soil to hold the little moisture or precipitation that does occur. The bright yellows and blues of the flowers against the earth tones of the sand and stones provide an appealing contrast of textures and colors.

A Butterfly and Hummingbird Garden

If you want to attract butterflies to your garden, choose flowers with contrasting colors and nectar-producing flowers. During the larval stage, butterflies use plants for feeding materials, so be careful not to use insecticides which could harm their chances of maturing.

There is really no secret to enticing hummingbirds and butterflies into your backyard landscape. All you need to do is provide an abundance of the plants that naturally attract them.

The best choices for a hummingbird or butterfly garden are native wildflower species. Native plants are suited to the local climate and therefore don't require intensive care. The bonus to a butterfly and hummingbird garden is that both of these creatures are nature's most efficient pollinators, creating excellent conditions for a perennial garden filled with bloom.

If possible, select a site for this garden within easy viewing from a favorite window. You'll discover the fascination of a backyard habitat that provides constant visual enjoyment.

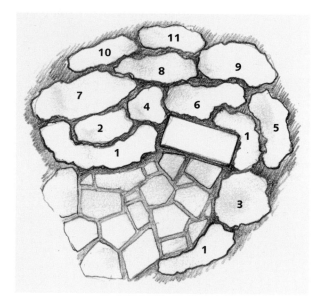

Plant List

1 Bluebells of Scotland
(*Campanula rotundifolia*)
2 Showy penstemon
(*Penstemon spectabilis*)
3 California fuchsia
(*Zauschneria californica*)
4 Colorado columbine
(*Aquilegia caerulea*)
5 Hartweg lupine
(*Lupinus hartwegii*)
6 Black-eyed Susan
(*Rudbeckia hirta*)
7 Blanket flower
(*Gaillardia pulchella*)
8 Butterfly weed
(*Asclepias tuberosa*)
9 New England aster
(*Aster novae-angliae*)
10 Purple coneflower
(*Echinacea purpurea*)
11 Thick-spike gay-feather
(*Liatris pycnostachya*)

Hummingbirds are particularly drawn to red flowers that point out or hang down. In addition to the flowers in this garden, other species that will lure them to your property include cardinal flower (Lobelia cardinalis), *standing cypress* (Ipomopsis rubra), *eastern columbine* (Aquilegia canadensis), *pinkroot* (Spigelia marilandica), *and scarlet sage* (Salvia coccinea).

A Living Wall

Native plants can often survive in conditions that are difficult or impossible for more finicky garden hybrids. Here is a stone wall that supports a cascade of color from small pockets of soil without requiring a great deal of extra care. The color combinations will change through the flowering season as the species bloom sequentially.

This drystone wall can provide a solution for a variety of landscaping challenges. You can use it as a natural screen to give privacy or to disguise an unsightly feature. Or you can construct it as a retaining wall to help terrace a sloping terrain.

Plant List

1 Shooting-star
(Dodecatheon clevelandii)
2 Blue-dicks
(Brodiaea pulchella)
3 Foamflower
(Tiarella cordifolia)
4 Prickly poppy
(Argemone hispida)
5 Linanthus
(Linanthus grandiflorus)
6 Desert marigold
(Baileya multiradiata)
7 Baby-blue-eyes
(Nemophila menziesii)
8 Tidy-tips
(Layia platyglossa)
9 Blazing star
(Mentzelia lindleyi)
10 Soapwort
(Saponaria officinalis)
11 Pasqueflower
(Anemone patens)

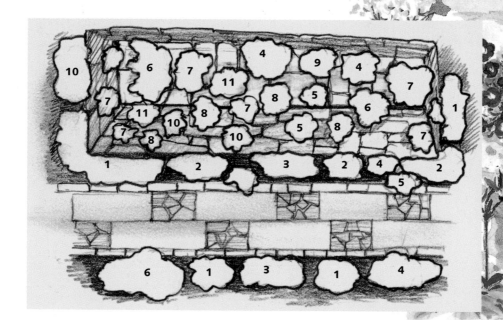

To create a living wall, remove a stone or brick from each place where you want to establish a plant. Fill the hole with nutrient-rich soil, plant a seedling, and water it well. It's all right for the seedling to be planted somewhat sideways—it will compensate as it starts to grow.

Hot courtyards or south-facing walls, which tend to be parched during the summer, may be ideal locations for plants native to arid regions. Here the moisture-loving species are placed at the base, where precipitation collects, and the drought-tolerant species are higher up.

CHAPTER 2

Planting and Propagating Wildflowers

*S*ometimes wildflowers are so suited to their environment that they spread rampantly once they begin to seed. • In time a single jack-in-the-pulpit *(Arisaema triphyllum)* can grow into a colony that covers the banks of a clear-running stream for hundreds of feet. Out in the wild, wildflower colonies should be left alone, except for an occasional gathering of seed, which should be done only with the landowner's permission. • There are three ways, however, to obtain plants for your own garden without disturbing the natural order of the plants: You can buy plants, divide or propagate established plants, or grow new plants from seed.

Plant Hardiness

American gardeners are often puzzled about why they can't produce traditional English gardens in their backyards. That's largely because they forget that England and Scotland are quite small in terms of geographic area (they both fit comfortably within the borders of New York State with plenty of room left over). Therefore, Britain's climate is fairly uniform from one end to the other. Also, it is warmed by the Gulf Stream flowing past its shores, which makes its climate more moderate than that in most of the United States and Canada. The wet English summers, with rain falling at least three days out of seven, and mild winters, in which the Thames River freezes over once every 400 years, are decidedly unlike American summers and winters. On one winter's day in February, the temperatures in the contiguous 48 states can range from 80°F in southern California and Florida to −45°F in the northern reaches of the great Midwest—a range of 125 degrees.

No wonder we can't have English gardens on this side of the Atlantic! Many of the plants that thrive in the British climate cannot tolerate either the intense heat or the bitter cold they encounter in the United States. About the only part of the country where the climate does resemble that of Britain is the Pacific Northwest. Gardens in the coastal areas of Oregon, Washington, and northern California can grow marvelous delphiniums and primulas and other stars of English gardens. The rest of us would do better to emphasize the beauty of our own native plants.

Because of the broad range of climates, topographies, and soil types in North America, the native flora varies greatly from one region to another. If you have ever moved from one part of the country to another, you have probably discovered that, although some of your favorite wildflowers can exist in both your new and your old gardens, a number of others cannot. No matter how much mulch you apply or how often you water, oconee-bells *(Shortia galacifolia)* never seem to last more than one season in the North. On the other hand, bunchberry *(Cornus canadensis)* thrives where winters are cold but the plant struggles from year to year and never does well where summers are very hot and humid.

So how do you choose native plants for your garden? First, ask other wildflower growers in your area about the plants they've had success with. Second, check with your county cooperative extension office for information, or visit a regional botanical garden to see what's growing there. Third, check the listings in any nursery catalogues you receive. Finally, do not be afraid to experiment to find plants that will flourish in your garden.

Obviously, common sense is important. Large evergreen-leaved tropicals will not survive a winter in Vermont. But you can experiment with plants that are not normally hardy in your area by making use of natural features in your garden, such as a grove of trees that provide protection from harsh winds, or microclimates (see pages 22 and 24). If you plant evergreen tropical plants near a house foundation or another location that is protected from the worst of the prevailing winter winds—and you mulch them well—sometimes they will survive.

When attempting to find protected locations on your property, keep in mind that cold air falls and warm air rises. Like water, cold air will flow down a slope and collect in pools at the bottom. A garden at the base of a hill or on the floor of a valley will be colder than a garden farther up the hill. If you live in a low spot, your garden is more likely to experience early frosts in fall and late frosts in spring.

If you garden in an area with plenty of snow cover, you can be more adventurous in your choices than a gardener in a region where temperatures plummet and the ground has no protective cover. People who grow wildflowers from the Himalayas are often surprised to learn that in their native habitat the plants are buried so deeply under yards of snow that their roots are scarcely, if ever, freezing.

Gardeners in southern regions have an opposite problem from their colleagues in the North. In southern gardens, plants may have difficulty enduring summer heat rather than winter cold. A spot at the bottom of a hill might actually be better for some plants in southern gardens than a warmer location above. Sometimes providing afternoon shade for plants will enable them to survive farther south than they normally would.

▼ Winter Heaving

The biggest problem many gardeners have with growing wildflowers (and perennials in general) is winter heaving. Without snow cover or mulch, the sun will often melt the frozen ground near the surface but the deeper earth will stay rock hard. A plant may have roots that extend through the melt zone into the frozen zone, and the alternate periods of freezing and thawing will pull roots right out of the ground and sometimes even break them. Once exposed to the open air, the roots dry out and die, or younger roots simply freeze to death.

To help prevent heaving, if you live in a part of the country where winter comes early, start your seedling wildflowers early in the year so that they have a chance to grow deep roots during their first season of growth. In autumn, after the ground has frozen for the first time, give the young plants plenty of mulch

to protect the roots. Once in frozen ground, they are better off than if left in open ground that could thaw and then refreeze. Also think about starting a nursery bed (see page 57) where plants have a good chance to develop before they are planted out in their final home in the garden.

Finally, be sure to walk through the garden periodically in winter, especially if there is no snow cover. If you find any plants heaved out of the ground, immediately push them back into the soil.

▼ Using Hardiness Zones

The best system developed so far for rating the hardiness of plants is that of the United States Department of Agriculture (USDA). USDA researchers divided the U.S. into regions of climatic similarity based upon the average winter minimum temperature as calculated from records kept over many years. Then they plotted the minimum temperatures that each region experiences onto a map. The resulting USDA zone map defines its plant hardiness zones by translating these average winter minimum temperatures into geographic terms. A map based on the most recent revised version of the USDA zones has been provided on page 127.

Use the map to find out which zone you live in. Keep in mind, however, that the map doesn't take into account all the factors that can cause the climate to vary widely within a given zone. In addition, since the zones are based on *average* winter temperatures, plants that are normally hardy in your location may not survive in a particularly cold or hot year. Finally, the zones reflect only the coldest temperatures usually found in a given region. Plant hardiness is also determined by the degree of heat a plant can tolerate.

Sources of Plants and Seeds

There are six ways to obtain wildflowers for your garden. First, you can grow many species from seed. Second, you can trade plants with other gardeners—one of the most memorable ways to start a garden. Third, you can collect plants in the wild, a practice that is frowned upon except under certain conditions (see pages 88–89). Fourth, you can send away to a number of mail-order nurseries located around the country (see pages 128–129). Fifth, you can seek out local nurseries and attend plant sales at botanical gardens and wildflower collections, and sixth, you can propagate vegetatively.

▼ Local and Mail-Order Nurseries

Whenever possible, it is wise to buy plants from local nurseries. If something goes wrong with a plant or you need advice, you can usually call on a local nursery to answer your questions. Discount companies may sell plants collected from the wild—even endangered plants—but reputable local nurseries either propagate their own plants or buy from dependable wholesalers. They also know which wildflowers will do well in your area and which will require special treatment in order to survive.

Although local sources are desirable, most of today's mail-order nurseries that specialize in wildflowers are knowledgeable growers who have turned the business of packing plants for long-distance shipment into an art. The catalogues of many of these companies contain a statement about the harm caused by taking plants from the wild. These firms readily

Venus's-flytrap (Dionaea muscipula) *is shown here growing and blooming in its only natural habitat, which consists of 16 counties in southeastern North Carolina and a few sites along the coast of South Carolina. Endangered, and thus protected by law, this plant prefers wet, sandy ditches; savannahs; and open bog margins.*

Venus's-flytrap is now an endangered species in its native habitats. But thanks to cloning, there is no need to gather wild material.

Seed Exchanges
The following groups make seeds available to members:

American Horticultural Society
7931 E. Boulevard Dr.
Alexandria, VA 22308
(703) 768-5700

American Rock Garden Society
P.O. Box 67
Millwood, NY 10546
(914) 762-2948

Canadian Wildflower Society
Unit 12A, Box 228
4981 Hwy #7
East Markham, ON,
Canada L3R 1N1
(905) 294-9075

Kansas Wildflower Society
The Herbarium
Kansas University
2045 Constant Ave.
Lawrence, KS 66047
(913) 864-3453

New England Wild Flower Society
180 Hemenway Rd.
Framingham, MA 01701
(508) 877-7630

acknowledge that all their plants are homegrown and propagated at the nursery.

▼ Seed Companies and Exchanges

Gathering wildflower seeds with an eye to protecting the environment isn't always easy. But with the increased interest in the environment, a number of small seed houses that specialize in both common and rare wildflowers and exercise the utmost care in gathering seeds for the marketplace have appeared across the United States and Canada. Rather than hiding behind complicated explanations about how they gather the seeds they sell, these companies tell you up front of their responsibilities to nature and to you, the customer.

In addition to commercial companies, a number of private plant organizations now sponsor seed exchanges or seed collections in which a large selection of seeds is available to members. Some of the larger organizations offering seeds are listed in the sidebar on this page. In addition, plant organizations in England often feature American wildflowers, since to English gardeners they have a definite cachet. And there are dozens of smaller organizations devoted to a single genus of wildflowers, like the American Penstemon Society, the American Calochortus Society, and the Desert Plant Society of Vancouver.

Today most regional botanical gardens feature wildflower gardens in their collections. At many gardens, volunteers gather seed that is later distributed to members for use in their own property.

Sources of Plants and Seeds CONTINUED

Commercial nurseries grow rows and rows of plants (these are Dianthus *spp.) to produce seeds. Try to buy your wildflower seeds and plants only from well-respected local nurseries.*

Perennial plant organizations, like the Hardy Plant Society, have also become sources of wildflower seeds because a number of species have made their way from wildflower gardens to become stars of the perennial border. Spiderworts *(Tradescantia* spp.*)*, butterfly weed *(Asclepias tuberosa)*, and even Joe-Pye weed *(Eupatorium purpureum)* began as native plants and are now grown in gardens around the world.

▼ Gathering Your Own Seed

Collecting your own wildflower seed can be a wonderful experience. When gathering your own seed, you are responsible for the entire process of growing a plant from beginning to end—and it's a great feeling. Generally if one or two gardeners collect seed from a large population of wildflowers, no harm is done, for there will still be plenty of seeds left to produce a new generation of plants in the wild. But if you are on park land or private property, you should find out beforehand if such collecting is allowed. And *never* collect seed from endangered plants unless you do it under the watchful eye of the owner, whether the garden or preserve is public or private.

Look for mature seed (usually the capsules are brown), and take only as much as you know you can use. Keep the seed dry, labeling the collecting containers with the date and the location of the seeding plants. After cleaning the seeds, store in a cool, dry place. Seed storage varies widely from plant to plant. By collecting and propagating plants from seed, you are helping to ensure the continued existence of our wildflower heritage.

1 *Shuck collected ripe seed capsules from wildflowers over a clean sheet of paper. Discard the hulls.*

2 *Pass the seeds through a fine screen to remove the grass or plant and insect debris.*

3 *Place the clean seeds on a fresh piece of paper, and carefully channel them into a clean, dry envelope. Seal the envelope tightly.*

4 *Label the envelope with the common name and scientific name and date. Store the seed envelopes in a cool, dry place until you're ready to sow them.*

Starting Plants from Seed

Seeds That Need Stratification

While a number of wild-flower seeds can be planted immediately upon ripening, many require stratification—a period of cold that breaks the seed's dormancy. Some of the more popular wild-flowers that need cold storage include common columbine (Aquilegia canadensis), 4 weeks; jack-in-the-pulpit (Arisaema triphyllum), 8 weeks; lily-of-the-valley (Convallaria majalis), 8 weeks; wild bleeding-heart (Dicentra eximia), 8 weeks; purple coneflower (Echinacea purpurea), 4 weeks; twinleaf (Jeffersonia diphylla), 8 weeks; Turk's-cap lily (Lilium superbum), 12 weeks; cardinal flower (Lobelia cardinalis), 8 weeks; perennial phlox (Phlox paniculata), 4 weeks; and fire pink (Silene virginica), 3 weeks. Consult a good reference book or an appropriate wildflower society to learn which seeds need stratification and for how long.

*B*uying seeds from a reliable source is a good way to start wildflowers. Seeds are abundant and much less costly than mature plants. Purchasing plants from a nursery can be quite expensive, especially if you want to buy a lot of them, and availability is sometimes limited. Also, starting from seed is a method that has long been held in high esteem, resulting in a wide variety of sources.

Wildflowers and other plants growing in suitable conditions will often reseed themselves if you do not deadhead the spent flowers. Dozens of little seedlings may pop up around creeping phlox *(P. stolonifera)*, for example, and you can transplant these volunteers to other locations. Transplanting self-sown seedlings is the easiest way to grow wildflowers from seed, but most gardeners prefer to purchase seeds for their wildflower gardens. Buying seeds, as opposed to

1 *To stratify seeds, place them in a container of moist vermiculite or sand, enclose the container in a plastic bag, and refrigerate for the appropriate period.*

relying on self-sowing, gives you more control of your garden, and a greater variety of plant choices.

Fortunately, once you obtain seeds, you can store them for an incredibly long time. Lotus seeds retrieved from an Egyptian tomb germinated in a 20th-century laboratory. You don't need an Egyptian tomb to save seeds for the wildflower garden, but a few safeguards will make them last far longer than they could if you left them lying around.

In order to reduce a seed's rate of respiration—yes, even seeds breathe—keep them in clean plastic bags, plastic film canisters, or tightly capped glass jars. Let newly collected seeds air-dry for a few days before placing them in storage. Seal the containers and label each with the name of the seed and date of collection. Keep the containers in the refrigerator—not the freezer—at a temperature between 34° and 41°F.

Not all seeds should be kept dry, however. Some are surrounded by a fleshy coating and must be stored in damp surroundings in order to prevent them from drying out. If they do dry out, they may go dormant for one or two years. The best way to store such seeds is to layer them with damp sphagnum moss in a plastic freezer container and refrigerate them along with your other seeds.

Finally, the seeds of some plants, such as bloodroot *(Sanguinaria canadensis)* and trillium, cannot tolerate any kind of storage at all. Unless these seeds are planted immediately, they are unlikely to germinate.

▼ Stratification

Some seeds will not sprout unless they pass through a period of cold—but not freezing—temperatures. The procedure of artificially duplicating the cold period provided in nature is known as stratification. This process can be used to break the dormancy of some

1 At planting time, prepare an improved soil mix for a wildflower bed. Sand, loam, and shredded peat moss are one all-purpose mix.

2 To hold the soil neatly in place, edge the area with stones. Carefully rake and level the bed before you begin planting.

3 Broadcast, or scatter, a wildflower seed mix by hand on a calm—not windy—day, spreading the seeds as evenly as you can.

4 Once the seeds are set, carefully use a rake or the flat side of a hoe to firm the soil.

5 Soon the seeds will germinate and a host of seedlings will cover the prepared earth.

6 After a few months the plants flower. This colorful garden has larkspur and coreopsis.

Starting Plants from Seed CONTINUED

wildflower seeds in order to start plants for the garden. The best way to stratify seeds at home is to place them in moist, but not wet, sand or vermiculite and then store the mix in plastic freezer bags in the refrigerator, ideally at a temperature between 34° and 41°F (although requirements vary). Usually two to eight weeks of cold storage is needed to break dormancy for wildflowers. Seed packets should contain information on the length of time needed for stratification.

The difference between seed storage and stratification is the amount of moisture the seed gets. Dry seeds remain inert in cold storage, but moist seeds that are undergoing stratification have the ability to clock up the days and know just when to begin to germinate.

Wildflower seed from commercial seed houses will come with notification if stratification is necessary. If you collect seeds yourself, research whether they require stratification. See the sidebar on page 52 for some plant seeds that need stratification.

▼ Starting Seeds

Many wildflower seeds benefit from spending the winter in a prepared bed, after which they will be ready to germinate in the spring. For these seeds the planting process should begin in January or February. Sow the seeds in flats filled with a mixture of equal parts good garden soil, sharp builder's sand, and crumbled compost or shredded leaves. Sprinkle the seed on top of the moist planting mix, then cover

with a thin layer of soil. To sow very fine seed, spread it as evenly as you can over the surface of the medium and leave it uncovered. Then carefully wet the soil until it is thoroughly moist but not sopping wet. Affix a label to the side of the container listing the time of sowing and the name of the wildflower.

Unless you are working with very rare or specialized seed, the planted flats should go directly outside for the winter, placed in a protected spot in the garden. The ideal place is a location facing north, where the light is good but the flats of seeds are protected from hot sun. If there are cats or other animals in your garden that might be tempted to dig in the soft soil, cover the flats with old wooden or aluminum screens.

If the weather is too severe or you don't have enough time to prepare an outdoor place for flats, you can start wildflower seeds indoors. The best time to begin is in early March, when the days are starting to lengthen again. Plant the seeds in a prepared mix as described above, using flats or smaller containers. Because you are dealing with wildflowers, you do not need to provide heat, as you do for many vegetable and perennial seeds to germinate. Put the containers of seeds in a place where the temperature is above freezing and the soil will gradually get warmer as spring approaches.

Growing Ferns from Spores

TROUBLESHOOTING TIP

A simplified method of growing ferns from spores— or plants from very small seeds—employs a brick. Spread a mix of clean sand and sterile peat or sphagnum moss over the top of the brick. Then place the brick in a pan with about 2 inches of water. The brick will automatically soak up just the right amount of water. As soon as the sand and moss mix is moist, spread the spores or seeds on the surface. Make sure there is always water in the pan. When prothalli form, thin them, and treat as directed in the text at right.

Ferns reproduce themselves by means of structures called spores. Most gardeners think that spores and seeds are the same thing, but from a botanical viewpoint they are worlds apart. A seed is the result of the fertilization of an egg cell in the plant's ovary by a sperm cell that enters in a pollen grain. When the seed is mature, it consists of a plant embryo surrounded by a seed coat and a food supply. A fern spore is a specialized cell that under the proper conditions will germinate to form a tiny prothallus—the fern's tiny, heart-shaped reproductive structure—which in turn produces both male and female structures on its underside. Sperm then swim in a film of water from the male organs (antheridia) to the female ones (archegonia) and produce a fertilized egg. Eventually, if conditions are right, this fertilized egg grows into a fern plant.

Once you know how the process works, it's easy to raise your own ferns from spores. The spores are normally found in spore cases (sporangia) on the undersides of fern fronds (people sometimes mistake these brown or black dots for insects or disease). Using a hand lens, watch for the spore case to begin to open, which usually indicates the spores are ripe. When this happens, remove the frond and set it on a piece of white paper. Make sure there is no moving air or the spores will blow away. The following day you should see millions of spores discoloring the paper.

Because the conditions that encourage spores to grow also invite various molds and fungi, keep your planting pots and tools as clean as possible. Assemble 3- or 4-inch clay pots that have been scrubbed clean. Fill the pots to an inch from the rim with a sterile soil mix of sharp builder's sand, potting soil, and milled sphagnum moss. If you aren't sure the mix is sterile, bake the pots and soil in an oven at 250°F for two hours (the odor will be unpleasant, so keep the windows open).

Soak the pots and mix in water until they are completely saturated, then drain off the excess. Cast the spores over the mix using a piece of folded paper. Put only one species in each pot and carefully label it. Then cover the pots with a sheet of glass or rigid plastic and put them in a dimly lit warm spot (between 65° and 70°F). Never put the pots in direct sunlight, and never let the medium dry out.

Many fern species will produce prothalli within a few days, but some may take a few weeks. You will see a green cast appear on the surface of the mix as the prothalli grow. In about three months they should be large enough for you to thin them out to about an inch apart. Condensation should produce enough water for the sperm to swim to the eggs, but you may have to mist the surface if the planting mix starts to dry out.

Tiny fern plants now begin to grow, appearing at the center of each prothallus. Once three or more fronds appear, transplant each fern to its own pot. It takes about two years for a plant to mature.

Caring for Seedlings

Getting the first green shoots of wildflower seedlings to grow into plants isn't as easy as it might seem. Remembering a few simple rules will increase your chances of success. First, never let seedlings suffer from a lack of water. Make sure the potting mix is always moist but not wet. Second, give the new little plants plenty of bright light but keep them out of the direct sun. Third, protect the seedlings from freezes and violent weather.

The first pair of leaves you will notice on a seedling are the cotyledon or feeder leaves. They usually look different from the leaves the plant will develop later. The new leaves that follow cotyledons are called true leaves because they have the shape characteristic of the particular plant. Transplant seedlings after they have produced several sets of true leaves.

▼ **Using a Cold Frame**

Gardeners who live in the North will find that a cold frame comes in handy for raising wildflower seedlings. A cold frame is basically a bottomless box that has a glass roof and sides protected from strong winds. You can make one by using concrete blocks for sides and old storm windows for a roof or by stapling plastic sheeting to a large piece of latticework. The cold frame creates a protected environment for plants, functioning like a miniature greenhouse.

To provide the maximum amount of sun for plants, position the frame to face south, with the back wall slightly higher than the front so that the glass cover sits at an angle. Wildflower seedlings can safely spend the entire winter in the cold frame. Leave the cover of the cold frame closed except on sunny days when the

1 *After seeds sown in flats have germinated and produced their first set of true leaves, it's time to transplant.*

2 *When transplanting seedlings to a convenient plastic cell unit, lift each plant by its leaves (not the stem) and support it under the root ball.*

3 *Set the containers of transplants in a shaded area, and carefully water with a soft spray from a hose. Keep the soil evenly moist but not soggy.*

outdoor temperature is above 40°F. Then open the lid partway to let in cool, fresh air, keeping the seedlings from overheating.

Once spring is on its way, remove the cold frame cover completely or leave the seedlings out in the open. If a freeze is predicted at night, replace the cover to protect the plants. Being in the open air toughens seedlings for life ahead.

▼ The Importance of Shade
Blistering sun can be a benefit to an old prickly pear (*Opuntia humifusa*) or a mature hedge of blue false indigo (*Baptisia australis*), but it could mean death to a baby cactus or most seedling plants. In nature, seedlings are usually sheltered by taller plants or grasses. The fledgling wildflowers in your garden also need protection from intense sun.

If the seedlings are in a cold frame, replace the glass cover with one made of old window screens when the sun is strong and the weather is warm. For plants in the ground, use window screens for shade covers, propping up the corners on concrete blocks. You can also stretch plastic shade cloth over metal hoops to make a tunnel or prop it like a small tent.

▼ Transplanting to Larger Containers
As seedlings grow, they must be transplanted to larger pots, a nursery bed, or the wildflower garden itself. Transplanting to individual pots is a good idea because it gives each seedling good-quality soil and a chance to grow roots under your supervision. If you use peat pots available from many nurseries, it's easy to move the plant to the garden later with minimal disturbance to the roots. You simply plant the pot and all (tear the sides of the pot to make it easy for the roots to grow through). Small plastic pots also

work well. The plants are easily dislodged from the pots at transplanting time, and the roots hold most of the soil together until they are ready to go into their new hole in the garden.

Wildflowers with long taproots do not take well to life in pots, as it's difficult to give the long root a container deep enough to allow it to develop properly. When taprooted seedlings outgrow the flat in which they were started, transplant them immediately to their permanent site in the garden.

Remember that moving seedlings requires special care: Even with gentle handling and patience, fragile feeder roots are likely to be damaged or torn off. Keep the soil evenly moist, but not soggy, until new growth signals that the plants have started to send out new roots and have settled into their new home.

▼ A Nursery Bed
A nursery bed is a small protected area where the soil is of good quality. It is a good place to transplant young seedlings, giving them a chance to grow larger without having to contend with too much sun, too much cold, and too little water. If you intend to raise a substantial number of plants from seed (pages 52–54) or cuttings (pages 70–77), put in a nursery bed. Place the bed close enough to the house so it's hard to ignore, and also site it near a water supply. Some gardeners use large cold frames as nursery beds, leaving the frames open in summer and closing them in winter. You will be amazed at the first year's growth when plants get the extra care available in a nursery bed.

TROUBLESHOOTING
TIP

Even though seedlings resent the direct rays of the hot sun, be sure to provide enough bright light to keep the plants growing straight and tall. If your light comes from only one source, make sure you move seedlings around so that the light eventually hits all sides of each plant.

Preparing Soil

EARTH·WISE TIP

If you remove an area of lawn to make room for a new garden, you can make compost from the sod you take up. The procedure is simple. In an out-of-the-way spot, pile up the pieces of turf in alternating layers, grass to grass, then root to root. Let the sod pile sit undisturbed for a year or two, and it will decompose into crumbly, fine-textured compost that can go into the garden to enrich the soil.

1 *Leaf mold is an excellent soil additive. Shred fallen leaves with a lawnmower or a leaf shredder.*

2 *Dump the shredded leaves into a wire bin, and let them decompose. Then dig the decayed leaves into the soil.*

*F*ew wildflower gardeners walk into a situation where great soil sits weedless under the high shade of a graceful old oak or hemlock—a site that needs only plants, a gardener, and a trowel to get started. Instead, there are usually low-growing tree limbs to be cut off, underbrush to be removed, and a healthy crop of weeds to be destroyed.

Once you've found the perfect spot for your wildflower garden, the first step is to remove all the existing vegetation. If your garden is being created from a lawn, dig up the sod and move it to a better place or compost it (see the sidebar on this page). If the area is full of weeds, you can avoid using herbicides by covering the ground with sheets of black plastic, pieces of old plywood (usually in 4- by 8-foot sheets), layers of newspapers, or thick layers of leaves to smother all the vegetation. Or try solarizing the weeds by

covering them with clear plastic. On sunny days the temperature under the plastic will get hot enough to cook the weeds and also destroy some of the weed seeds in the upper layer of soil.

Whatever material you use to cover the weeds, begin the process in late spring and leave any covering in place for two months or more. When the plants are dead, remove the covering and let everything dry for a few days. Then the soil can easily be tilled and the drying vegetation plowed or dug under to add organic matter to the soil.

Even after the existing plants have been removed, plenty of weed seeds will remain in the soil. If allowed to germinate, they will immediately compete with, and in many cases overtake, your newly established wildflowers.

After the initial preparation is finished, give those remaining weed seeds a chance to germinate. Wait about a week after a good soaking rain or a heavy sprinkling, then till the soil to a depth of only 1 inch. This will kill the weed seedlings that responded to the water but will not unearth newly planted seeds lying at a greater depth.

▼ Improving the Soil

Few gardeners are blessed with perfect soil. Although in wildflower gardening the goal is to grow plants that are naturally suited to the type of soil available in your garden, you can still take measures to improve the texture and fertility of the soil without changing its basic character. Improving the soil will allow you a greater choice of plants and make it easier for plants to thrive. You can begin amending the soil once the garden area is cleared of vegetation.

Never forget that any soil can be improved. Gardeners digging through heavy clay bemoan the hard labor required before planting. But the rich, crumbly black soil found in our forests began the same way many years ago. What turned the dense clay into crumbly loam was simply leaf mold. Over generations, all those fallen leaves slowly enriched the woodland soil. The typical forest floor consists of soil that is the envy of many gardeners. You can have the same kind of soil in your woodland wildflower garden, and it won't take generations.

In these beds prepared for wildflowers by the New England Wild Flower Society, the well-prepared acid and humusy soil is slightly raised to promote drainage from severe rains.

Preparing Soil CONTINUED

About pH

The pH scale is used to measure the relative acidity and alkalinity of the soil. It ranges from 0 to 14, with 7 indicating soil that is neutral. Soils with a pH less than 7 are acid; those above pH 7 are alkaline.

Swamps and bogs have a high percentage of peat and are very acid. In humid regions, including most forests, the soil is moderately acid to slightly alkaline. Arid regions range from moderate to strongly alkaline.

It is important to test your soil pH; some wildflowers can tolerate a range, but others are very particular. Most garden centers stock an inexpensive pH tape that changes color to indicate the degree of acidity.

In the fall all woodland gardeners (even those whose woodland consists of just a few trees) should gather fallen leaves, either from their own backyards or from those of neighbors. Many municipalities give away leaves collected by road crews and park groundskeepers for use in composting. Shred the leaves before they get too wet from rain and begin to pack down. You can run over the leaves several times with a shredding lawn mower or put them through an electric or gas-powered leaf shredder. If you don't wish to purchase a shredder, you can rent one for a day or two (see the step-by-step photos on page 58).

Spread the shredded leaves over the soil, and till or dig them in. You will begin to see results very quickly: the soil will be lighter by the next growing season. Continue tilling shredded leaves into the soil every autumn, and in several years your garden soil will be as rich and dark as forest soil. Clay soils are usually rich in nutrients (often containing far more than the typical wildflower needs), and by adding compost or shredded leaves, you open up that fertile soil and allow wandering roots to penetrate easily.

▼ Matching the Soil to the Plants

By studying the physical properties of a plant, you can learn a great deal about its environmental demands. Evergreen plants with taproots, such as yuccas, survive in less-than-perfect soil because their roots can go deep in search of both water and nutrients. Prickly pears *(Opuntia* spp.*)*, with their ability to store water in their thick leaves, do well in sandy, usually dry soil. Plants from the desert also usually prefer soil with a neutral to alkaline pH.

One look at the thick, horizontal roots of a typical violet and you can see why this particular plant can take abuse and imperfect soil and still spread like

wildfire. In contrast, gaywings *(Polygala paucifolia)*, which are small and delicate in appearance, need a rich, acid, humusy soil.

These examples drive home the point that plants should be matched to their soil preferences. Plants that are found on beaches in the wild need excellent drainage. Alpine wildflowers that originate high in the mountains will grow in little more than shredded rock—and they, too, must have perfect drainage. Any water standing around the roots is fatal to these plants. Prairie plants, on the other hand, like a good but very deep soil. They need to send their roots far underground in order to survive drought and occasional fires.

Giving wildflowers in the garden the same kind of soil found in their natural habitats goes a long way toward ensuring they will thrive. For some plants it is essential. Indian-paintbrush *(Castilleja* spp.*)*, for example, has a symbiotic relationship with certain bacteria that live in the soil around its roots in the wild. Without the bacteria the plants seldom live long, making them very difficult to grow successfully in the garden.

Before purchasing any wildflowers—either seeds or plants—for your garden, have your soil tested for pH and nutrients, and learn as much as you can about its characteristics. Then choose plants suited to the type of soil you have. If you don't know the soil needs of a plant you want to buy, investigate by reading garden books, consulting a wildflower society, or asking a reputable nursery before you purchase it.

Planting Meadow Gardens

EARTH·WISE TIP

If you garden in a part of the country that is subject to heavy rains, cover newly seeded areas with one of the new lightweight floating row covers or "garden blankets" that allow light and air to penetrate but prevent heavy raindrops from dislodging the soil and disturbing seeds.

A wildflower meadow, like any other kind of garden, requires site preparation. Follow the procedures discussed on pages 58–59 to clear a site for a meadow. The seedbed must be smooth and weed-free, as any existing weeds will compete with wildflowers for water, sunlight, and nutrients. If allowed to grow unchecked, they will eventually take over your garden. You need to keep the area free of weeds for the first two or three years after seeds are sown to allow your wildflowers and grasses to become established. Then the wildflowers should be able to hold their own against aggressive weeds.

▼ Exchanging Lawns for Meadows

The easiest and fastest way to create a meadow garden is to trade in an existing lawn by removing the top 3 inches of grass and soil using a sod cutter (this tool is easy to rent if you don't own one). You can then garden the area immediately, remembering that the soil level in the new garden will be lower than the existing land. Or you can buy new topsoil to replace what's been taken away. If you do, make sure you purchase good, weed-free soil rather than common fill, which can introduce a host of problems.

The other way to clear away the grass is by cultivation. This entails digging up the soil with a tiller at least two or three times in sessions spaced about one week apart. If your existing lawn consisted of rhizomatous perennial grasses, it may take up to a year of repeated tilling to eliminate them entirely.

There are wildflower seed assortments available for different kinds of meadow gardens, including annual and perennial wildflower mixes for different climates and areas of the country and even special mixes for the desert, where water is scarce. Before you buy a wildflower seed mix, contact your state native plant society and your county cooperative extension agent to find out about any invasive plants that should not be planted in your area.

For most gardens in the United States, the best time to sow a meadow is spring. Most reliable seed companies suggest that when sowing newly turned land, you use 10 pounds of seed per acre (5 pounds of grass seed and 5 pounds of wildflower seed). If the land already has existing trees and shrubs, sow just 5 pounds of seed per acre. For denser growth, you can use up to 15 pounds of seed per acre on flat land and up to 20 pounds on steep slopes. To sow a meadow on an average city lot of 50 by 150 feet, you need about 1½ pounds of seed. Sow seeds as evenly as possible over the surface of the prepared soil. See the step-by-step photos on pages 62–63 for more information on how to plant a meadow.

Meadow plants may take up to three years to establish themselves. Weed new meadows well so that young plants receive enough soil nutrients and sunlight.

Planting Meadow Gardens CONTINUED

1 If you want to replace part of a lawn or field with a meadow garden, begin by mowing the area.

2 The next step is to use a sod cutter or a quickly biodegradable herbicide to kill the existing grasses and weeds.

5 After cultivating, use a rake to level the soil and break up any remaining clumps.

6 Broadcast the wildflower seeds by hand. To keep the soil loose, move across the bed on a board.

3 *After a safe interval of time, cultivate the now-empty area with a hand cultivator if the area is small.*

4 *If the area is too large to cultivate by hand, work up the soil with a rotary tiller.*

7 *Once seeds are sown, carefully rake them in. Don't step on the soil.*

Transplanting Outdoors

More seedlings are lost through improper transplanting than from any other cause. Imagine a seedling growing happily in a flat or pot in a cold frame, its tender roots and rootlets pushing their way easily through a porous, crumbly planting mix. The potting mix contains just the right amount of nutrients, and the gardener supplies plenty of water when needed. If necessary, the seedling is even given shade from the sun.

Then the time comes to transplant the seedling to the garden. You dig a small hole in the middle of wide-open territory, remove the seedling from its pot of nice soil, plunk it into the hole in the garden, give it a spritz of water, and walk away, figuring the plant can now fend for itself. A week or two later you return to find all the seedlings are gone and wonder why. Such problems can be avoided if you give new transplants some special treatment until they settle into their new home. A little extra care now will result in strong, healthy plants that will need less fussing over later.

Whether your wildflowers are small homegrown seedlings or larger plants from a local nursery, be sure to take the following steps when transplanting. First, prepare the soil properly with enough humus to hold moisture and still permit good drainage. Then, after you install the seedlings, make plenty of water available—at least until the plants form new rootlets in a week or so. Keep the soil evenly moist, but not sopping wet, during this period. Then you can slack off a bit, but you must continue to provide water when plants need it, especially if there is no rain.

1 *A lightweight garden fabric will protect a newly seeded hillside meadow. Anchor the cover with stones or pins, and remove it when seedlings come up.*

You must also provide shade from a potentially searing sun until plants become accustomed to conditions in the garden. Shade is especially critical for seedlings that were started indoors, as they can suffer sunburn if exposed to intense sun too abruptly. Give them shade for their first few weeks in the garden. Several methods of shading seedlings are discussed on page 57.

▼ Spring versus Fall Planting

Generally speaking, the best time to transplant wildflower plants to their permanent spots in the garden is late summer to early fall. Even though growth slows at the plant's crown in autumn, the roots continue to

From the alpine meadows of the Pacific Northwest comes avalanche lily (Erythronium montanum), a species with white petals instead of the yellow ones more common to this genus. Seedlings of this species thrive with plenty of leaf mold in the soil.

grow until the ground temperature approaches freezing—and that can be for a long time, even in the colder areas of the country. Gardeners in warm climates should plant later in fall, when the summer heat begins to abate.

The mild weather of fall is more congenial for plants than the up-and-down temperature swings that occur in spring in many places. By the time the next spring rolls around, your fall-planted wildflowers will already be settled in with good root systems, ready to meet the weather head on.

▼ What to Expect from Seedlings

The wildflowers you are raising from seed are, for the most part, perennial plants. Usually they will not bloom the first year. Instead of producing flowers, they direct all of their energy toward growing roots and establishing themselves for future growth and reproduction. Depending on the species, some wildflowers, such as trilliums, won't bloom for five to seven years after planting. Gardeners tend to want quick gratification for their efforts. But with wildflowers, patience is a virtue. Give them the time they need to establish themselves in your garden.

Remember to clearly label the seedlings as soon as they begin to grow. Otherwise you might mistake your treasured plant for the inevitable weeds that will also sprout, and inadvertently yank the seedling from the garden.

Planting Bulbs

When placing wildflower bulbs before planting, scatter the bulbs at random in order to achieve a natural look. If, after planting, you want to record the names on an unobtrusive label, insert a wooden dowel topped with a numbered tack (the kind used to match up storm windows) into the ground, then make a list of the numbers and their plants.

Among the most popular wildflower bulbs are trout lilies *(Erythronium spp.)*, camass *(Camassia spp.)*, wood leeks *(Allium spp.)*, spider lily *(Hymenocallis caroliniana)*, and Canada lily *(Lilium canadense)*. Many of them must be treated differently from herbaceous plants.

Because the bulbs are concentrated food sources, the plants will perform the first year even if they are not matched to the site and soil in which they are planted. But immediately afterward, when the bulb can no longer nourish them, the plants will go into a decline if they lack the right growing conditions. Plant wildflower bulbs in soil that is rich, humusy, and well drained, unless the instructions that come with the bulb direct otherwise. (Also consult the encyclopedia beginning on page 96.)

The rule of thumb for determining the depth of planting for a bulb is to plant it roughly two and a half times deeper than its own diameter. Thus, a lily bulb that measures 2 inches across should be planted 5 inches deep.

When planting wildflower bulbs, try to plant in groups rather than scattering single bulbs far and wide. A group or mass of bulbs planted together creates a more striking visual effect than single specimens. In fact, the larger the number of bulbs used, the better the show. If you are planting a number of bulbs, you might want to try a bulb planter—a special tool that makes deep, round holes. You simply plunge it into the soil as deep as you need, pop in the bulb, and replace the soil.

Some bulbs are magnets for hungry chipmunks and mice. And even though moles are meat eaters, they can dislodge bulbs while digging tunnels and cause them to dry up from root loss. If you are planting bulbs that are favorite foods for wildlife or might be disturbed by moles, enclose the bulbs in small cages made of hardware cloth for easy protection. It takes a bit longer to accomplish the planting, but it works.

After the bulbs bloom, they produce leaves that nourish the bulb. Don't remove ripening bulb leaves until they dry up and fall back naturally, even though they sometimes look messy. That way the bulbs will get all the food they need for next season's display of flowers.

The Turk's-cap lily (Lilium superbum) *bears majestic flowers on stems up to 8 feet high, often with more than 30 blossoms in a cluster. It is well suited for woodland or shady gardens.*

Planting in Special Situations

Plants for Seaside Gardens

There are many salt-tolerant native grasses, including sea oats (Uniola paniculata), a native of the Southeast but hardy as far north as zone 7; northern sea oats (Chasmanthium latifolium), hardy from zones 5 to 9; and European dune grass (Ammophila arenaria), hardy from zones 5 to 10. The native bearberry (Arctostaphylos uva-ursi) does well in an open and sandy environment and makes an effective ground cover.

Wildflowers that adapt to seaside gardens include blue false indigo (Baptisia australis); butterfly weed (Asclepias tuberosa); California poppy (Eschscholzia californica); most of the goldenrods, especially the seaside goldenrod (Solidago sempervirens); the field asters; coreopsis; and a selection of sedums and sempervivums.

Planting wildflowers in meadows and woodlands is relatively straightforward, but other situations require more specialized treatment.

▼ Planting in a Sand Dune

It's easy to obtain successful results from seaside gardening if you heed a few cautions. Salt spray is a problem for some plants, but if you walk most beaches—in areas not trampled by millions of bare feet—you will find a surprising number of wildflowers and native shrubs in residence, especially on sand dunes. Two major problems need to be solved: improving the poor sandy soil and providing windbreaks to soften strong winds and buffer salt spray. But if you do this, wildflower gardening near the sea can be a fascinating adventure.

Drainage is rarely a problem with sand and enriching the soil is fairly easy by adding plenty of compost. As sand and coastal soil conditions vary widely, a formula for how much organic material to use is not practical. You must work in enough compost to hold moisture for the eventual use of your plants, especially those not adapted to growing directly on the beach. Compost, well-rotted livestock manure, and leaf mold are all good sources of organic matter.

▼ Planting in a Desert

Like seashore gardeners, desert gardeners must deal with poor soil. In addition, desert soils are often extremely alkaline because the low rainfall allows mineral salts to build up in the soil. Before you can plant, you may need to flush the soil with clear water that is not too soft (that is, not high in sodium and other salts). Consult your county cooperative extension office for advice.

The next step for desert gardeners is to work organic matter into the soil so that the choice of plants for the garden can be expanded. Otherwise, choose plants that are native to or have naturalized in your area; these have adapted to tolerate the existing soil.

▼ Planting in a Bog

There are a couple of ways to garden with bog plants. To grow just a few plants, bury a plastic dishpan with the top edge about 6 inches beneath the soil surface. Then fill it with good garden soil laced with plenty of humus. Once you install the plants, soak the dirt thoroughly, and eventually the buried pan will fill with water, providing what the plants need for active growth. To create a larger bog, you can use the same waterproof liners that are used to make garden pools (see pages 15–17). Install the liner as you would if you were making a pool, but in this case excavate the soil to a depth of only 1 foot and replace all the soil after the liner is in position. Water the soil until it becomes good and soggy.

▼ Planting Water Lilies and Deep-Water Plants

Native water lilies can easily be grown in a 6-inch flowerpot. The soil should be regular garden soil, heavy on the clay side. Mix in a handful of water-lily fertilizer or use the tablet form. Saturate the soil, then plant the root so that it is covered to the crown. Add an inch of very small stones or gravel on top of the soil to keep the dirt from washing out of the pot. Gently submerge the pot in the water. In a shallow pool, set the pot on the bottom so that there is about a foot of water above the plant crown. In deeper pools you can set the pot on a concrete block or bricks to get the correct level.

Planting In Special Situations CONTINUED

EARTH•WISE TIP

To grow a water plant or a bog-loving plant in a dry area, try burying a plastic pail. Fill it with water for water plants or with a water and soil mix for bog plants. Then put the selected plant in its pot in the water or in the water and soil mix.

1 To give plants a good start in a difficult site, let seedlings, like these from the cardinal flower, grow into larger plants before setting them out.

2 If the seedlings become crowded (as they are in the previous photo), transplant them into individual pots so they have room to develop larger root systems.

3 Several weeks later the cardinal flowers are in bloom; this is a good time to transplant them to an appropriate place in the garden.

4 Here the blooming plants are installed around the margin of a pond. Place the plant at the same depth as it was growing in its pot, and keep the root ball intact.

1 Desert soils are extremely alkaline and poorly drained. Make raised planting areas, like these beds edged with local stone, in order to improve the drainage.

2 Fill the beds with an improved-soil mix containing sand for increased porosity and better drainage. The improved soil will help plants adapt to a desert environment.

3 Dig holes before removing plants from containers. Handle cacti with heavy gloves and a wrapping of newspaper to keep spines out of your fingers.

4 Set each plant in a hole, firm the soil around it, and water. Finish your garden by covering the soil with a neat stone mulch.

Vegetative Propagation

TROUBLESHOOTING TIP

Success with softwood cuttings is often a matter of timing. To determine the right time, try the snap test. Bend the stem you wish to use for cuttings between your thumb and forefinger. If the stem snaps, the tissues are probably in the right condition for rooting. If the stems bend or do not break clean, the cutting will probably not root.

*I*n addition to growing wildflowers from seed, you can enlarge your plant collection using other, faster methods that are collectively called vegetative or asexual propagation. With these techniques new plants are made from the old by dividing the rootstocks or by taking cuttings from the leaves, stems, and roots of various plants and getting them to grow into new plants. Except in a few cases, the variations found in seedling plants are not found in vegetatively propagated plants; the new plants are genetically identical to their parent.

▼ **Stem Cuttings**

Softwood stem cuttings are the most common method used for vegetative reproduction. Softwood cuttings are taken from the green stems found in the first year of a plant's growth, before the stem begins to harden into mature tissue. Late spring or early summer is the best time to start cuttings because at that time plants are rich in food stored in their cells. Among the wildflowers that can be reproduced from stem cuttings are yarrows *(Achillea* spp.*)*, asters *(Aster* spp.*)*, bellflowers or harebells *(Campanula* spp.*)*, phlox *(Phlox* spp.*)*, cinquefoils *(Potentilla* spp.*)*, soapworts or bouncing bets *(Saponaria* spp.*)*, pincushion flowers *(Scabiosa* spp.*)*, and fire pinks *(Silene* spp.*)*.

Plant growth, like animal growth, is regulated by hormones that stimulate development. Often cuttings will respond better and faster to conventional rooting methods when they are given an application of a plant growth hormone. This compound is available in powder form at all nursery and garden centers. To use rooting hormone, pour out a small amount of the powder and dip the cut end of a cutting in the powder before you set it into the growing medium. Be sure to follow package instructions and treat these

1 *Take 3- to 5-inch-long stem cuttings of healthy shoots in late spring or early summer. (Phlox stolonifera is shown here.) Cut just below where a leafstalk meets the stem.*

4 *Set the cuttings in holes about 2 inches deep in pots of moist, sterile medium. Make sure the bottom of each stem touches the bottom of the hole. Firm around the stem.*

2 *Remove any flowers and damaged leaves. With clean, sharp pruners, carefully remove the leaves from the bottom third or half of the stem cutting.*

3 *If you want, dip the bottom of the cutting in rooting hormone powder poured from a package. Discard any excess after planting the cuttings.*

5 *Label containers of cuttings with the name of the plant, the flower color, and the date. Enclose the containers in a plastic bag, or cover them with glass to retain humidity.*

6 *Place the cuttings in a warm location with good light. A cold frame in partial shade or with shade netting over the lid is a good spot if the weather is not too warm.*

Vegetative Propagation CONTINUED

When taking cuttings, always take them from a healthy plant. Experiments have shown that softwood cuttings taken from weak plants in poor soils will be slower to form roots than cuttings taken from healthy plants.

chemicals with care. Discard any leftover portion of the powder when you have finished; do *not* return it to the package, as it could contaminate the rest of the powder with bacteria.

If only a few plants are to be propagated from stem cuttings, the best method is to use a combination of small pots (2¼-inch diameter) and quart-sized food storage bags. With a sharp, clean knife or razor blade, cut off a healthy stem between 3 and 5 inches long. Take the cutting just below the point where a leaf-stalk joins the stem. Remove any damaged leaves and all flowers. Then neatly take off the bottom leaves so that the stem is free for at least 2 inches. Fill a pot with a sterile growing medium or moist sphagnum moss. Be sure the medium is moist but not soggy. Roots need oxygen in order to form, and when stems are set into wet soil, they often rot from lack of air.

Using a pencil, make a hole about 2 inches deep in the potting medium. Insert the cutting (after applying rooting hormone if needed), making sure that the base of the stem touches the mix at the bottom of the hole. Next, firm the medium around the stem and carefully put the whole setup in a plastic bag, sealing the top. Set this miniature greenhouse in a warm—but not hot—place with good light but not in direct sun. In about two weeks, give the cutting a slight tug to check if the rooting process has started. If it hasn't, pull out the cutting and check for rot. If it looks healthy, try the rooting procedure again.

▼ Root Cuttings

One of the easiest ways to expand your wildflower collection is by taking root cuttings. Among the plants that can be propagated by root cuttings are bleeding-heart *(Dicentra* spp.*)*, evening primrose *(Oenothera*

1 *Prickly pear can be propagated from leaf cuttings. Wear gloves to protect your hands when taking the leaf cuttings.*

4 *When the individual pots of prickly pear plants are firmly rooted, you can transplant them outdoors.*

2 *Place the leaf cuttings in an upright position in a propagation medium of potting soil mixed with sand.*

3 *When rooting has commenced, move the cuttings to individual pots, again using soil mixed with sand.*

5 *Use the new plants to fill in bare spots in an established prickly pear colony or to start a new colony.*

Vegetative Propagation CONTINUED

spp.), butterfly weed *(Asclepias tuberosa)*, St.-John's-
wort *(Hypericum* spp.), Stokes's aster *(Stokesia* spp.),
wild ginger *(Asarum* spp.), phlox *(Phlox* spp.), plume
poppy *(Macleaya cordata)*, globe thistle *(Echinops*
spp.), and mullein *(Verbascum* spp.).

In the fall dig up a plant selected for propagation.
If you want only a few plants, use your spade to pry
part of the plant out of the soil and cut off the roots
you need. If you want a lot of plants, you can use the
entire root system for cuttings. Choose the thicker
roots that are closer to the plant's crown, usually
about $\frac{1}{10}$ inch in diameter. Spread the roots out and
cut them into 4- to 6-inch lengths.

Make a root propagation bed using a wooden flat.
Fill the flat with a mix of equal parts of sharp
builder's sand, good garden soil, and chopped sphagnum or peat moss. Then take the root cuttings and
place them in rows about 2 inches apart on the surface of the rooting medium. Cover with $\frac{1}{2}$ to 1 inch
of medium, and water well.

Keep the flats in a cold frame over the winter,
mulching well after the first few frosts. The following
spring new shoots will appear. When they reach a
height of 3 inches, transplant the plantlets to the nursery bed or individual pots.

▼ Leaf Cuttings

Nature never planned on leaf cuttings as a major way
to create plants, so the process works for only a few
wildflowers. But coralbells *(Heuchera* spp.), stone-
crops *(Sedum* spp.), prickly pears *(Opuntia* spp.), and
possibly others can be reproduced by this method.
Using the mix described for making regular cuttings,
fill a pot or a flat. Then place the individual leaves,

1 *To divide a crowded clump of crested iris or
other plants suited to this method of propagation, first lift the clump from the garden.*

5 *Once rooted, the divisions of crested iris are
ready for planting in another part of the wildflower garden.*

2 Pull or cut apart the clump of rhizomes and roots into smaller sections. Discard the older, inner portion of the clump.

3 Make sure that each division contains healthy roots as well as top growth or some dormant growth buds.

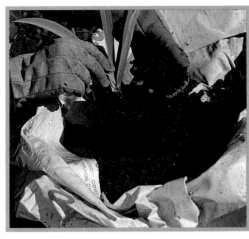

4 Pot the divisions in a clean, moist soil mixture that contains plenty of humus. Work quickly so roots don't dry out. Then water well.

6 On a cloudy day, set out the new irises in the garden at the same depth they were before. After planting, give each iris plenty of water.

7 If set out in late summer or early fall, the new divisions of crested iris will bloom the following spring.

Vegetative Propagation CONTINUED

with a bit of stem attached, on top of the mix, leaving an inch or so between each leaf. Keep the pot or flat in a warm (65°F) place, and make sure the mix doesn't dry out. (See the photos on pages 72–73.)

▼ Division

Division is an easy way to provide more plants for the wildflower garden, but it works only with plants that have multiple crowns, that is, plants that form clumps. Early in the year, before new growth begins, is the best time for dividing because plants are primed to grow in spring. If your growing season is long enough, you can divide fall-blooming plants in the spring and spring bloomers in the fall, so you won't delay their flowering.

Start by lifting the entire mother plant out of the soil. Then pry the plant apart with a cultivating fork or break it into smaller pieces using a sharp spade. Make sure there are some roots left with each piece, plant them immediately, and water well.

Plants that arise from underground rhizomes, such as great Solomon's-seal *(Polygonatum commutatum)*, bloodroot *(Sanguinaria canadensis)*, or Virginia bluebells *(Mertensia virginica)*, can be increased in number by cutting the thickened roots into 2-inch pieces. Make sure each piece has an eye or shoot. Let the wound heal overnight, then plant in the same mix used for root cuttings, covering with an inch of soil.

Some plants, like golden star *(Chrysogonum virginianum)*, spread by underground stems called stolons (similar stems growing on top of the ground are called runners). At the tip of the stolon, a new small plant will form that has only a few feeder roots because the majority of the nutrients are provided by the mother plant. If new plants are cut away and moved to a nursery bed, they will be ready for the garden in about one growing season.

Violets (Viola *spp.*) *spread by themselves and can be propagated by division.*

Coltsfoots (Galax urceolata) *can also be divided. The leaves are used by florists in cut-flower arrangements.*

The cultivated white form of dwarf crested iris (Iris cristata 'Alba') is easily grown from seed or by division of the rhizomes after flowering.

▼ Layering

Almost any plant that has a creeping style of growth and branches that can be bent to the ground without breaking can be rooted in a process called layering. Take a living stem and cover it with a lump of soil weighted down with a small stone—make sure that the growing tip is still out in the open air. Usually within one growing season new roots will form and a new shoot will appear. When the new growth is obvious, cut the stem from the mother plant and allow it a full season to form new roots, then move it to a new spot in the garden or to the nursery bed.

▼ Offsets

Many herbaceous wildflowers, such as sneezeweed *(Helenium autumnale)*, cardinal flower *(Lobelia cardinalis)*, hens-and-chickens *(Sempervivum* spp.*)*, and yuccas *(Yucca* spp.*)*, form new shoots of foliage around the mother plant. If these offsets have roots and are cut from the parent with a sharp knife, they can become new plants. A number of bulbous wildflowers produce small bulblets next to the mother bulb. When the bulb is dormant, it can be lifted from the ground and the new bulblets removed and set out in a nursery bed until they mature.

▼ Lily Scales

Lilies are true bulbs, but unlike daffodils and onions, they are made of individual pieces of tissue called scales. Remove a few scales from a dormant mother bulb and push them to about half their length into a soil mix used for rooting cuttings. Over the course of a growing season, they will form new little plants. The tiny bulbils that are found along a lily stem can also be planted like seeds, and they, too, should show signs of growth in one season.

Virginia bluebells (Mertensia virginica) *bear porcelain-blue bells of great beauty. Grow new plants from seed or by division as the foliage dies down.*

In early spring bloodroot (Sanguinaria canadensis) *displays its pristine white flowers. Grow the single form from seed or singles and doubles by division of the rootstock.*

CHAPTER 3

Caring for Wildflower Gardens

*a*s every gardener knows, weather can be unpredictable. One winter may bring freezing rains and ice storms, while the next is marked by record snowfalls. • In some summers there is abundant rain, making fields and lawns fresh and green. In other years protracted droughts leave perennial gardens browned and short of bloom. • But no matter what the weather brings, every year the fields and forests are aglow with wildflowers, which have been able to exist in adverse weather conditions for thousands of years. • Tough as they are, however, wildflowers need a little help when they are moved into the confines of the home garden, especially when they start out as seedlings or newly rooted cuttings. This chapter outlines how to care for your wildflower garden year after year.

Watering

How to Water a Garden

Most perennial gardens need about an inch of water a week, but a well-established wildflower garden can get by on much less. The need for water will vary according to the temperature of the air and how fast the air is moving. High winds speed evaporation. Also, shallow-rooted plants need more water than those with deep roots.

Overhead sprinklers are the least efficient way to water because much of the water evaporates in hot sun or warm air or is blown away by winds. Trickle or drip systems that supply water directly to the root zone are best. Drip systems use plastic or rubber tubing with tiny holes that allow water to seep slowly into the soil.

All of a plant's major underground growth activity is concentrated at the tip of each root, which is furred over with thousands of thin, soft hairs. Their function is to soak up water and nutrients from the soil. In some plant species, the fine root hairs are tough enough to pass between particles of even closely packed soil without breaking. But a crumbly, porous soil with plenty of space between individual particles is best, making it easy for the root to take in the water and air it needs. Adding organic matter to heavy clay soil lightens the texture, so roots can penetrate more easily.

You can tell a lot about a plant's watering needs from its roots and its leaf structure. Once they have established themselves, taprooted plants such as yuccas *(Yucca* spp.*)* and butterfly weed *(Asclepias tuberosa)* are relatively drought resistant because they can absorb water and minerals from deep underground. Plants with a fibrous root system spread out many thin and branched roots to occupy a wide expanse of shallow soil. Fibrous roots must be able to capture water as it begins to percolate into the ground and to absorb everything they need before the water sinks deeper into the ground and out of reach. If there is a drought, the fibrous-rooted plants will suffer before deeper-rooted plants. Instead of giving them a quick drink with the hose every day, encourage deeper rooting in fibrous-rooted plants by watering them deeply but not frequently. For information on the moisture needs of individual plants, see the encyclopedia beginning on page 96.

Be sure to consider the moisture retentiveness of your soil. Soil is a complex mixture of inorganic matter (mostly derived from eroded rock) and humus, an organic material that results from the decomposition of plant and animal tissue. The inorganic materials include sand, silt, and clay, and mixtures of these substances are called loams. A sandy loam contains a greater proportion of sand particles, and a clay loam has more clay particles. Humusy soil has substantial amounts of organic matter.

The more humus any soil contains, the greater is its ability to hold water. Sandy soils hold very little water—it just runs between the large grains. But if you add compost to sandy soil, you can expand the choice of plants that will survive in your garden.

Clay soil is so tightly packed with tiny sticky particles that after a heavy rainstorm it becomes waterlogged, depriving plant roots of oxygen. You often find standing water at the surface of clay soil. While some tough plants, like the obedient plant *(Physostegia virginiana),* have root systems that thrive in these conditions, more delicate plants, such as meadow rue *(Thalictrum* spp.*),* have a tough time surviving in thick clay soil. If you have clay soil, you can expand your plant choices by adding humus. This will make the soil drain better while still holding water for long-term use by the roots (the humus particles act like tiny sponges); it will also allow for the free exchange of air.

Eventually, if you chose your plants wisely, the wildflowers in your garden will be able to get by on their own, with supplemental watering needed only during prolonged dry spells. Until they are established, however, it is important to provide plenty of water to the plants that need it. The first rule is to water well when you do water. Use enough to soak into the soil and deep down into the ground. Short periods of surface watering force roots to grow up to the wet surface rather than down into the dirt. When the top layer of soil dries out, the roots quickly die.

Weeding

*I*n his classic book, *The Gardener's Year*, the playwright and gardener Karel Capek called weeds "pests [that are] creeping, or rooted a foot deep in the earth; if you want to pull them out they break off at the root." Unfortunately, this last remark is all too is true. Weeds by their nature are programmed to take over the world. For an attractive wildflower garden, you must learn how to manage weeds.

Nature makes sure that weed seeds do not drop right at the foot of the parent plant, where they would find only exhausted soil. Thistle and dandelion seeds, for example, fly on feathery wings and cover great distances before they land in your garden. Other weed seeds are brought into the garden on the hairs of animals or even on your own clothes. Still others enter your domain in the digestive systems of birds and other small animals.

The price of a weed-free garden is continual vigilance. Although there are weed killers on the market, using these chemicals in a wildflower garden seems a contradiction. After all, nature uses no herbicides in the prairies and forests untended by gardeners.

Check your garden often for weeds, and pull them up, roots and all, before they become established or have time to go to seed. Use mulches to cover bare soil (see pages 82–83). When you do weed, try to pick a time after a rain when the plants have dried off but the soil is still loose and wet. Grasp the weed stem close to the ground and pull up (be sure to remove the entire root). If necessary, use one of the many weeding tools on the market to give you leverage with strong roots. Then if the weeds have not yet gone to seed, add them to a compost heap.

One of the benefits of wildflower and meadow gardens is that weeding can be kept to a minimum. Once established, most wildflowers can easily cope with the majority of weeds.

Mulching

Starting a Compost Pile

To begin a compost pile, select an out-of-the-way spot in your garden where you can pile up grass clippings, various kitchen scraps (vegetables and fruits only), and vegetation gathered from raking.

In a bin or pan, make alternating layers of vegetation separated by soil, shredded leaves, or even sawdust. Cover kitchen waste with shredded leaves before adding the next layer. Cut up large items, such as watermelon rinds. Add grass clippings only in thin layers, or they will mat down and turn smelly.

Once a week or so, turn the pile with a pitchfork to allow decomposition to proceed at an even pace. If the weather is dry, you will need to water the pile occasionally to keep it moist. Compost is ready to use when it is dark brown, crumbly, and earthy smelling.

Mulch is an important component of the wildflower garden. The application of mulches to the soil surface slows down the rate of water evaporation, prevents the germination of many weed seeds, and keeps the soil surface from developing a hard crust. The soil remains loose and crumbly all season, able to soak up water when it rains instead of losing a substantial amount to runoff.

Depending on the materials used, mulches can improve the appearance of a wildflower garden by making the setting look more like something nature would produce than something designed and planted by a gardener. After all, in nature's garden the soil surface is usually covered by plant debris or other natural material. The key to choosing a mulch that will look natural in your wildflower garden is to pick mulch materials that are similar to materials found in the habitats where your plants grow in the wild.

For woodland gardens and for shady wildflower gardens in general, the best mulch is a layer of shredded leaves. A leaf mulch echoes the look of the layer of leaf litter that accumulates on the forest floor, and the leaves—like other organic mulches—gradually decompose and add organic matter to the soil. At the end of the garden year, you can dig the mulch into the soil, then add more leaves to protect plants during the winter.

To prepare leaves for use as mulch, rake them up from your yard in the fall or get them from your neighbors or from your city or county road maintenance department. Then use a commercial leaf shredder to shred them before they get too wet in autumn rains. If you are not shredding large amounts of leaves, you can rake them into shallow piles and run over them several times with a power lawn mower. Use the crushed leaves as a mulch over the winter and

1 *Pine needles are one of the best mulches for a woodland garden. They are acidic, slow to decompose, and provide perfect drainage.*

as a summer mulch too. Spread a layer 6 inches deep in winter and 1 to 2 inches deep in summer.

Wood chips and shredded bark also make natural-looking mulches for woodland gardens. You will probably need to renew the mulches every spring to keep them from getting too thin. Before you spread the new mulch, scatter some nitrogen fertilizer over last year's mulch to replace the nitrogen taken from the soil by wood products as they decompose. Use manure, cottonseed meal, or a commercial fertilizer with a high nitrogen ratio.

A mulch made of pine needles is especially popular in the Southeast. It looks natural, lasts a long time, and allows water to pass quickly through to the soil. But pine needles are acidic and should only be used to mulch plants that like a low pH.

2 *Be sure to use a mulch of natural materials with wild-flowers. Shredded leaves or leaf mold are good choices in shady or woodland gardens.*

3 *A no-maintenance gravel and stone mulch looks perfect near a pond or streamside garden, in a rock garden of alpine plants, or in a desert garden.*

TROUBLESHOOTING TIP

Whenever possible, use a mulch that allows the free passage of air. Peat moss, for example, is unacceptable as a mulch because it tends to form a nonpermeable crust. If you are using a mulch around the base of a tree, keep it a couple of inches away from the trunk. If mulch remains in direct contact with the trunk, mice could hide there in winter and gnaw the bark.

Stone mulches are excellent in rock gardens and around drought-resistant plants. A mulch of pea gravel, for example, will keep mud from splashing onto delicate rock garden plants, especially during heavy rains. You can also mulch plants with pebbles or with larger stones gathered from the property.

Layers of black plastic are often used by gardeners as mulch, but they hold too much heat and deflect too much water to be recommended for a wildflower garden. Black plastic mulches also look decidedly unnatural. Instead, you might try thin layers of newspaper as a mulch, but cover them with a more aesthetic material.

Most garden centers sell a variety of mulches, including wood or bark chips in small and large sizes, cocoa bean hulls, buckwheat hulls, marble chips, construction gravel, and turkey grit (a crushed granite used by turkey farmers and available in three grades). You may also find commercially prepared compost and mixtures of organic matter combined with cedar chips to give the material a pleasant odor.

Avoid using baled peat moss as mulch. Peat has little available organic content and makes a very poor mulching material. It quickly packs down, then dries out so completely that it repels water and keeps it from soaking into the soil. In addition, peat can act as a wick and actually draw water out of the soil. And it blows around when it's dry. If you want to use peat moss in your garden, work it into the soil; do not spread it on top as mulch.

Caring for a Meadow

Don't confuse a meadow garden with a wild garden. A meadow garden is under the control of the gardener, and the flowers and grasses grow there by choice rather than chance. A wild garden is a place where nature alone makes the choices.

A meadow garden usually contains a greater variety of wildflowers than would be likely to grow in a single field in the wild. Choices include New England and New York asters *(Aster novae-angliae* and *A. novi-belgii)*, lance-leaved coreopsis *(Coreopsis lanceolata)*, Queen-Anne's-lace *(Daucus carota* var. *carota)*, pale and purple coneflowers *(Echinacea pallida* and *E. purpurea)*, queen-of-the-prairie *(Filipendula rubra)*, gay-feather *(Liatris* spp.*)*, beebalm *(Monarda didyma)*, black-eyed Susan *(Rudbeckia hirta)*, and goldenrod *(Solidago* spp.*)*. Turn to pages 128–129 for some suppliers of wildflower seeds for meadows.

Although meadows don't require a lot of maintenance, especially when they are well established in their third or fourth year, weed control is very important when a meadow is young. Begin cutting back or pulling out the weeds when they reach a height of 8 to 12 inches, and keep a continual watch. If you let the weeds go, they will crowd out your wildflowers. At the end of the first garden season, stop cutting back the weeds. They can remain over the winter to provide protection for the smaller wildflowers growing in their shadows.

Caring for the meadow garden is easier in the second year, but there is still work to do. In early spring, when the soil thaws, mow any plant left standing from the first year—weed or wildflower—to the ground. This mowing helps in the germination of any seeds left over from the previous year, and it causes most of the wildflowers to grow even thicker in the second season. Carefully remove the cuttings with a bamboo rake to avoid uprooting any seedling plants.

Later in the season, when the meadow is up and growing, you may want to mow a pathway through it as shown in the photos on page 85. A neatly mowed path will allow you to stroll through your meadow to watch birds, bees, and butterflies at work or to pick some flowers for a bouquet. A path also imposes a sense of order, demonstrating to dubious neighbors that it is indeed a garden and not wild.

During a meadow garden's first year, annuals (or perennials grown as annuals), such as the showy evening primroses (Oenothera *spp.)* *and Texas bluebonnets* (Lupinus texensis) *shown at right, provide color while the slower-growing perennials are becoming established.*

1 To further enjoy a field of blooming wildflowers, you need a path through the meadow that lets you walk without causing damage.

2 Use a sickle bar or heavy-duty mower to cut a path through the plants. Be sure that the blades are clean and sharp before you begin.

**TROUBLESHOOTING
TIP**

When cutting grasses for a meadow garden, be sure to match the mower to the job. Lawn mowers are a poor— and sometimes dangerous— tool to cut most field grasses. For cutting small fields on a yearly basis, buy or rent a sickle bar. Keep all blades used for cutting grasses as sharp as possible.

3 Never follow a straight line when mowing a path through a meadow. A meandering course is more interesting and looks more natural.

4 The finished pathway can be mulched with pine needles or crushed leaves. Or, if you don't mind the extra maintenance, you can replant it with lawn grass.

Pest Control

EARTH·WISE TIP

Among the many different types of pesticides, horticultural oils have been around for a long time and are still very effective. These highly refined petroleum oils smother insects by blocking the air passages that allow them to breathe. The new, lighter oils are used to control whiteflies, mites, and many other plant pests, yet they are safe to use around people and pets. Always follow directions when using horticultural oils.

Except for an occasional nipped leaf or chewed flower, wildflowers are usually not troubled too much by pests, and they seldom suffer from wilts, blights, or other diseases. If your wildflower garden starts out with good soil and adequate watering, and you remove any diseased or decaying plant material as soon as it appears, you are on your way to growing healthy plants. Most of your problems will revolve around insects and possibly slugs, depending on your location and the type of garden you have. Both can be controlled without chemical sprays.

Slugs are snails without shells. They are often found in woodland gardens, where they chew ragged holes in foliage and flowers. They leave silvery trails of slime on the ground as evidence of their passage. You can easily remove them by sneaking into the garden at night with a flashlight and catching them at work. Pick them off the plants (wear gloves) and throw them into a can of soapy water or sprinkle table salt on their bodies.

Japanese beetles are a scourge in many gardens, especially sunny ones in summer. They can be controlled with bait traps, but be sure you follow the instructions on where to place them. If you hang the traps right in the garden, they may attract Japanese beetles from all over the neighborhood and leave your garden in worse shape than it was before. Japanese beetles are slow to react, although they will fly away or hop off plants when sufficiently disturbed. If you work quickly, you can pluck them off a leaf and squash them between your fingers (again, wear gloves) or drop them in a can of soapy water.

Insects such as spider mites and aphids can be controlled by washing them off plants with a strong jet of water from the garden hose or by spraying them with a solution of liquid dishwashing soap, then washing

1 *Deer and other animals can be a problem when summer ends and food becomes scarce. Protect a small bed with a cage of chicken wire, hardware cloth, or plastic netting.*

the foliage in about 10 minutes. Or try one of the new insecticidal soaps to fight these pests.

Two garden insecticides are made from plants. Pyrethrum is made from the flower heads of the pyrethrum daisy *(Tanacetum cinerariifolium),* but it has two drawbacks: Sunlight reduces its effectiveness, and it kills some beneficial insects. Rotenone is made from the roots of the tuba plant *(Derris ellliptica),* but it also kills helpful insects and can irritate human lungs. Use these insecticides only as a last resort.

Finally, if you learn to accept some damage to your plants, your gardening life will be easier. Only take action when pests or diseases cause significant trouble that could actually weaken plants. After all, you want a natural look in a wildflower garden, so a few tattered leaves seem appropriate.

Controlling Invasive Plants

*I*f you have no personal knowledge of a plant's potential for invasion, and your nursery or seed catalogue or the encyclopedia section of this book does not warn of any dangers from a particular wildflower, it probably won't present any problems in the garden. A few plants, however, should be mentioned here: oriental bittersweet *(Celastrus orbiculatus)*, Japanese honeysuckle *(Lonicera japonica)*, kudzu *(Pueraria lobata)*, English ivy *(Hedera helix)*, and poison ivy *(Rhus radicans)*. All are highly invasive under the right conditions, and the first two should never be considered in a garden setting unless you are willing to work at keeping them in line. With that in mind, you should also know that Japanese honeysuckle is less rampant in poor, arid soil and can actually be quite useful in such situations. And although English ivy can be a real problem in warmer climates, it takes a while to get going, usually giving the gardener time to root up unwanted plants.

Poison ivy is spread by birds that eat the seeds in the early fall. When you spot poison ivy, put on a pair of latex gloves and pull it out. In a wider area, repeated mowing will eventually get rid of it. Remember that even the dead roots and branches of poison ivy can give you a rash if you touch them.

Occasionally a weed becomes too persistent to control by hand pulling. Although herbicides should not be used unless they are absolutely necessary, in this instance you may need to resort to one. There are many weed killers on the market, so read the labels carefully before you buy one. Products based on a glyphosate formula are quickly biodegradable and do not linger in the environment in a toxic form. If

Oriental bittersweet (Celastrus orbiculatus) *looks like its native American counterpart* (C. scandens) *but is more invasive and aggressive; it crowds out other plants in its path.*

you follow the package directions explicitly and aim carefully when you apply them, these products should kill the invading plant without causing undue harm to the gardener, local pets and wildlife, or the garden.

You might also investigate a new kind of weed-killing tool that uses a propane gas tank to produce a very tightly focused flame. The flame is used to burn out the offending weed without hurting the plants next to it.

Saving Plants

**TROUBLESHOOTING
TIP**

*When collecting plants from
the wild, you can protect the
roots well by wrapping them,
along with some soil, in
damp newspaper. Then place
the plants in plastic bags and
keep them in a cool place out
of direct sun.*

All across the country developers are developing and
builders are building. The result is a continuing
assault on the natural world in general and wildflowers in particular. So if you see a wildflower habitat
sitting in the path of earthmovers and bulldozers, ask
permission to save the plants. Then get out your shov-
els, trowels, and plastic bags; enlist some help if possible; and set out to rescue as many as you can. You
may also need to save plants on your own property,
moving them out of the way of a flood, for example,
or taking a few prized specimens with you for your
garden at a new home.

Another reason for moving wildflowers is if another gardener offers you one of his or her plants. Other
gardeners can be a valuable source of wildflowers for
your collection. To meet fellow gardeners, simply join
a local wildflower club or plant society.

*Fall-blooming asters carpet the fields of rural America with
their starlike white, blue, or purple flowers. They can easily be
moved from the field to the wildflower garden.*

▼ **Guidelines for Moving Wildflowers**

Even though many wildflowers are tough and easily
withstand climatic difficulties when established in the
wild or the garden, some have an Achilles' heel when
it comes to moving. Here are some guidelines to
observe when moving wildflowers:

▼ Try to move wildflowers after their blooming period is over and the plants are winding down for their
late fall and winter dormancy.

▼ Younger plants are easier to move than older ones.

▼ Move wildflowers on a cool, cloudy day. And
plan on transplanting them during rainy, but not
stormy, weather.

▼ Keep wildflower roots moist at all times—never let
them dry out.

▼ Take plenty of soil with the plants (keeping as
much around the roots as you can), and quickly move
them to the proper-size plastic bag or other container.

▼ Try to replant the same day you dig up plants.

▼ Watering is especially important. Keep the soil
evenly moist for several weeks (or longer in dry conditions) as the plants adjust to their new home.

1 You may need to move a plant in your own garden. Here a cardinal flower is rescued to be reused in another part of the garden.

2 Using a good, sharp shovel, dig around the cardinal flower, keeping plenty of soil around the roots, and remove the plant from the hole.

3 Set the plant in a clean pot, and if you cannot transplant it immediately, set it in a shady place and keep it moist.

4 Dig a hole in the plant's new home, making sure you break up the soil in the bottom of the hole with a shovel or a trowel.

5 Remove the plant from the pot, set it in the hole, water well, then firmly press the soil around the roots. Water again as needed.

Saving Plants CONTINUED

**TIMESAVING
TIP**

If you are going to dig in the wildflower garden, use landscaping flags to mark the position of wildflowers that fade and disappear after blooming, such as Virginia bluebells (Mertensia virginica), *or camas lilies* (Zigadenus spp.). *Stores that sell engineering and surveying supplies stock landscaping flags, made of heavy wire topped with small white, yellow, green, black, or red vinyl flags.*

The rosy paintbrush (Castilleja rhexifolia) *pictured here was found in Yellowstone National Park. No matter how beautiful, no plant should be taken from government parklands.*

Cutting and Preserving Wildflowers

Plants for Cutting

Wildflowers suitable for cutting include aster (Aster *spp.*), *beard-tongue* (Penstemon *spp.*), *beebalm* (Monarda *spp.*), *black-eyed Susan* (Rudbeckia hirta), *butterfly weed* (Asclepias tuberosa), *cardinal flower* (Lobelia cardinalis), *coltsfoot* (Galax urceolata), *columbine* (Aquilegia *spp.*), *coralbells* (Heuchera sanguinea), *dame's rocket* (Hesperis matronalis), *various ferns, gay-feather* (Liatris *spp.*), *goldenrod* (Solidago *spp.*), *various grasses, Jacob's-ladder* (Polemonium *spp.*), *larkspur* (Delphinium *spp.*), *lily* (Lilium *spp.*), *lupine and bluebonnet* (Lupinus *spp.*), *meadow rue* (Thalictrum *spp.*), *obedient plant* (Physostegia virginiana), *oxeye daisy* (Leucanthemum vulgare), *purple coneflower* (Echinacea purpurea), *Queen-Anne's-lace* (Daucus carota *var.* carota), *rose verbena* (V. canadensis), *sage* (Salvia *spp.*), *sneezeweed* (Helenium *spp.*), *sunflower* (Helianthus *spp.*), *Virginia bluebells* (Mertensia virginica), *and yarrow* (Achillea *spp.*).

Many wildflowers, ferns, and grasses can be enjoyed indoors as well as out in the garden. You can use some of them freshly cut in bouquets and arrangements. Others dry well, and still other wildflowers can be pressed and dried, then used in craft projects.

Some good choices of wildflowers to cut are given in the sidebar on this page. The best time to cut them is early in the day, when the dew has dried but the flowers are still fresh, firm, and full of moisture. By afternoon, especially on a hot day, the plants will have lost some of their moisture to the air, and the flowers may be somewhat flaccid. Limp flowers will not hold up well in a vase.

Use sharp tools for cutting flowers, and cut only the healthiest, most perfect blooms. In many cases flowers are best cut when the buds are partially open and showing color but not fully open. Cut flowers are still alive after you cut them and will continue to mature. If you cut them fully open, they are more likely to droop or drop their petals in a few days. Some flowers, however, are fine if you cut them when completely open. Experiment with the flowers available to you to determine the best cutting times.

Take a bucket of cool water out to the garden with you when cutting flowers. With your knife or flower snips, cut cleanly through the stem, leaving no ragged edges, and immediately plunge the cut end of the stem into the bucket of water. Putting the stems in water right away will help your flowers last longer in the vase because the stems can continue taking up water.

Another important aid in getting the maximum vase life from your flowers is to condition them before you arrange them. To condition flowers, stand the stems up to the base of the flowers in a bucket of cool water in a dark place. Leave the flowers in the dark for three to four hours or overnight.

Conditioning causes the stomata on the undersides of leaves to close, so less water vapor will be transpired from the plant tissues into the air and the flowers will stay fresher longer. Seal the ends of stems that ooze sap by dipping them in boiling water or holding them over a candle flame.

Keep the vase as free of bacteria and contaminants as possible. Scrub it with soapy water, rinse thoroughly, then fill with fresh, cool water. Add a few drops of liquid chlorine bleach to the water. Remove all leaves that would be underwater in the vase, or they will foul the water.

▼ Drying and Pressing

There are three basic methods of saving wildflower blossoms for dried bouquets or other craft applications: air-drying, drying in a desiccant such as sand or silica gel, and pressing.

Air-drying is the simplest method. Sometimes a fresh bouquet will sit in a vase, and over the course of a few weeks the water will dry up and the flowers will dry themselves beautifully, especially in a heated room in the wintertime. Unfortunately, there is no guarantee that this method will work every time, and it is much better to air-dry your flowers by more reliable methods.

Start with freshly picked blossoms and immediately remove all the leaves from the stems. Drooping flowers, especially of grasses, can be tied into loose bundles, then hung upside down from hooks or hangers in a dark, dry, well-ventilated room. An airy attic is generally a better place to dry flowers than a basement, which tends to be damper. Because stems shrink as they dry, be sure the bundles are firmly tied. Better yet, fasten them with rubber bands, which will tighten as the stems shrink.

Cutting and Preserving Wildflowers CONTINUED

Plants to Dry or Press

Wildflowers suitable for drying or pressing include aster, beebalm, black-eyed Susan, butterfly weed, coralbells (Heuchera *spp.*), *seedpods of false indigo* (Baptisia *spp.*), *various ferns, fire pink* (Silene virginica), *fireweed* (Epilobium angustifolium), *gay-feather, goldenrod, various grasses, seedpods of irises, Joe-Pye weed* (Eupatorium purpureum), *larkspur, lily, seedpods of lotus* (Nelumbo lutea), *meadow rue, pods of milkweed* (Asclepias syriaca), *mist flower* (Eupatorium coelestinum), *mullein* (Verbascum *spp.*), *purple coneflower, Queen-Anne's-lace, queen-of-the-prairie* (Filipendula rubra), *rattlesnake-master* (Eryngium yuccifolium), *sage, sunflower, violets* (Viola *spp.*), *and yarrow.*

1 *When gathering wildflowers for an arrangement, carry a basket or a bucket of water with you and always use sharp, clean scissors.*

2 *Bring the cut wildflowers to a nearby table or other clean area with plenty of room to lay out the flowers according to their size and color.*

3 *Arrange the flowers in a complementary vase filled with fresh water. Stoneware and crockery are especially attractive containers for wildflowers.*

4 *The finished arrangement will be not only a beautiful addition to your home but also a compliment to your skills as a wildflower gardener.*

If you have lots of flowers, you may wish to build or buy a drying rack. One simple design is a rectangular wood frame with several horizontal slats or bars from which bunches of flowers can be hung. Or staple chicken wire to a wooden frame and put the flowers directly on the wire with the stems sticking through.

Some flowers hold their color and form better when dried in a desiccant material. For large flowers, such as lilies, and for flowers with many petals, such as asters, drying in a desiccant works best. You can use clean, well-washed beach sand, or silica gel, which is sold at craft shops and florist supply houses. Silica gel dries flowers faster and preserves the most color. It is the same material you find in little envelopes packed with expensive electronic equipment to prevent damage from moisture. It is somewhat expensive, but you can reuse it over and over. When the blue crystals turn pink, they have absorbed all the moisture they can. Spread them on a cookie sheet and place in a warm oven until they turn blue again. Then store them in an airtight container.

To dry flowers in a desiccant, cut off the flower stem right below the flower head. (Later you can use green florist's wire to create imitation stems for the flowers.) If you are using sand, you can dry the flowers in an open wooden box. If you are drying in silica gel, you will need an airtight container with a tight-fitting lid.

Spread a layer of desiccant about an inch deep in the bottom of the container. Lay the individual flowers on top of the material. Place flat flowers, such as asters, face down. Put spiky flowers, such as salvias, on their sides. Set large flowers, such as lilies, upright or on their sides. Be sure the flowers do not touch one another.

Gently sprinkle the desiccant over the flowers, working it carefully in between the petals and in all the empty spaces. To hold the shape of a flower that is tubular or another form with empty space inside, you will need to fill the inside of the flower with desiccant. In any case, try to place the desiccant so that the flower retains its original shape as it dries. Cover the flowers with an inch or two of desiccant, making sure no petals or other parts protrude. Close the container (if it has a lid) and set it in a cool, dry, airy place. After several days, gently brush away some of the desiccant to see if the flowers are dry. You want the flowers to be papery but not brittle.

For some craft projects, you may want to use pressed flowers. In the past people often pressed flowers between the pages of a book, as you may have discovered after buying an old volume at a rummage sale. Even after 100 years, the petals still have color and the leaves are green. To speed up the process, you can either buy or make a flower press consisting of thin wooden boards with holes drilled at the corners. Place flowers on layers of blotting paper (available at office supply stores and craft shops) between boards, and then tighten the screws in the holes to make a sort of sandwich.

TROUBLESHOOTING TIP

Dried flowers tend to be fragile. Some require a protective coating to keep the flowers from shattering. Use a spray varnish, which also gives the plant material a sheen or gloss, or try a floral fixative spray. Another problem is that the stems may break or bend. You can buy green 28- to 30-gauge wire from craft shops to reinforce or lengthen the stems. Wrap the stem and the wire together with green florist's tape.

Regional Calendar of Wildflower Care

 Spring

 Summer

COOL CLIMATES

Spring

- Divide crowded clumps of summer- and fall-blooming wildflowers in early spring, as soon as the soil can be worked. Divide ferns before new fiddleheads uncurl.

- Mow meadow gardens to remove last year's dead plants.

- Clean up the wildflower garden early in the season, removing dead plants and other debris. Pull weeds.

- Sow seeds in a cold frame or directly in the garden.

- Start a nursery bed in a sheltered location to provide special and slow-growing plants with extra care until they are large enough to go into the main garden.

- Give newly transplanted wildflowers some shade and plenty of water as they settle into the garden.

- If you plan a new garden, test your soil for its pH.

- Start a compost heap.

Summer

- Deadhead spent flowers if you do not want the plants to self-sow, and if you do not want to collect seeds to plant next year.

- If the weather is dry, mulch plants that will suffer from the lack of moisture. If necessary, water these plants.

- When mulches on paths in woodland gardens grow thin, add fresh mulch.

- Turn the compost heap every week or two, and don't allow it to completely dry out.

- Take cuttings to start new plants.

- Mow a path through meadow and prairie gardens so that you can stroll through and enjoy the plants.

- Weed newly planted meadow and prairie gardens until the plants become established.

- Look around the garden and cut back any plants that are invading their neighbors.

WARM CLIMATES

Spring

- Divide crowded clumps of summer- and fall-blooming wildflowers in late winter or early spring. Divide ferns before new fiddleheads uncurl.

- Mow meadow gardens to remove last year's dead plants.

- Clean up the wildflower garden early in the season, removing dead plants and other debris. Pull weeds.

- Start a nursery bed in a sheltered location, where special and slow-growing plants can be raised until they are ready to go into the main garden.

- Give newly transplanted wildflowers shade and plenty of water as they settle into the garden.

- Turn the compost pile every week or two, and don't allow it to completely dry out.

- Deadhead spent flowers if you don't want the plants to self-sow and if you don't want to collect seeds.

- Weed newly planted prairie and meadow gardens until the plants become established.

Summer

- Continue to deadhead spent flowers.

- If the weather is dry, make sure plants get enough water.

- When transplanting new plants to the garden, do so early in the season, before the worst of the hot weather arrives, and do it early in the morning.

- Take cuttings to start new plants.

- Continue to turn the compost pile every week or two.

- If you want to keep cool-season prairie grasses from going dormant, give them plenty of water.

- Add fresh mulch where it has grown thin in the garden.

- Mow a path through prairie and meadow gardens so that you can stroll through on cool evenings and enjoy the plants.

- Look around the garden and cut back any plants that are invading their neighbors.

Fall

- In all but the northernmost locations, start a new wildflower garden now to let the plants become established before winter.

- Unless you live in the Far North, divide and transplant spring- and summer-blooming wildflowers that need it.

- Move deeply rooted plants when they go dormant.

- Dig compost into the soil.

- Shred fallen leaves for winter and summer mulches.

- Set out seeds that need stratification to overwinter for germination in spring. A cold frame is a good place for this.

- Build a cold frame if you don't already have one.

- Collect seeds as they ripen; clean and store them.

- Be sure the garden is well watered going into the winter months.

- Start a new wildflower garden by sowing seeds or planting transplants. The plants can then establish themselves and put on a better show next spring.

- Divide and transplant crowded clumps of wildflowers.

- Move deep-rooted plants when they go dormant. Mark their locations while they are still growing actively so you'll know where they are when they die back.

- Work compost into the soil.

- Continue to collect seeds as they ripen. Clean and store them.

- Continue to weed as needed.

- Continue to deadhead spent flowers.

- Sow hardy annual wildflowers directly in the garden.

 Winter

- Plan new gardens you want to start next year.

- Create pathways through woodland and other gardens.

- Order seeds and plants early from mail-order nurseries for the best selection.

- Check for plant roots heaved out of the ground by alternate freezes and thaws. Gently push any exposed roots back into the soil, and cover with mulch.

- Take a walk through the winter garden.

- Build a cold frame and use it to start seeds of cold-tolerant plants.

- If the soil freezes where you live, be sure the garden is well watered when it does.

- If you plan a new garden, test the soil for pH.

- Start a compost heap if you don't already have one.

- Clean up the garden, removing spent annual wildflowers, dead plants, and other debris. Make new paths where you want them.

- Order seeds and plants early from mail-order nurseries to get the best selection.

- In late winter, prepare soil for new garden beds.

This table offers a basic outline of garden care by season. The tasks for each season differ for warm and cool climates: Warm climates correspond to USDA Plant Hardiness zones 8 through 11, and cool climates to zones 2 through 7. Obviously, there are substantial climate differences within these broad regions. To understand the specific growing conditions in your area, consult the Zone Map on page 127. Also be sure to study local factors affecting the microclimate of your garden, such as elevation and proximity to water.

Wildflowers & Native Plants for American Gardens

This section provides concise information on more than 150 plants recommended for wildflower gardens. The plants have been selected on the basis of beauty, adaptability, and availability. To find a plant of a certain height or with flowers of a specific color, check the Growth Habit or Flower Color column. If you need plants for a dry or moist spot, look under Growing Conditions. Or study the photos, read the descriptions, and then decide which plants will grow well in your garden.

▼ About Plant Names

Plants appear in alphabetical order by the genus name, shown in bold type. On the next line is the most widely used common name. The third listing gives the complete botanical name: genus, species, and if applicable, the variety. Occasionally an alternative botanical name is listed below this in parentheses.

Common names vary, but botanical names are the same everywhere. If you learn botanical names, you'll always get the plant you want from a mail-order nursery or local garden center. One gardener's green-and-gold may be another gardener's golden star, but both gardeners will recognize the plant if they know its scientific name: *Chrysogonum virginianum*.

When several species in a genus are similar in appearance and cultural needs, they are listed together in a single entry. If, however, a genus contains two or more vastly different species, each of the recommended species is given a separate entry.

The second column of the chart provides a brief plant description. Look here to see if the wildflower or native plant is an annual or perennial, what its leaf or flower shape is, and whether its form is creeping, upright, shrubby, or vining.

▼ Flower Color

The color dots following each description indicate the color *family;* they are not literal renderings of the flower color. A plant given a pink dot might be pale blush pink, clear pink, or bright rose pink.

▼ Time of Bloom

Bloom time is given by season and may vary from one year to another according to climate, weather, and growing conditions. A plant that grows over a broad range, such as eastern columbine *(Aquilegia canadensis)*, will bloom several weeks earlier in the southern part of its range than in cooler climates.

▼ Growth Habit

The Growth Habit column lists the height and spread a plant may reach at maturity. This information is expressed in ranges to account for the natural variability in plant growth.

▼ Hardiness

Plant hardiness is generally an indication of the coldest temperatures a plant is likely to survive. But many plants also have limits to the amount of heat they can tolerate. In this chart hardiness is expressed as a range from the coolest to the warmest zones where the plant generally thrives. The zones are based on the newest version of the USDA Plant Hardiness Zone Map, shown on page 127.

▼ Growing Conditions

The last column summarizes the best growing conditions for the plant, including its light, moisture, and soil requirements.

		Flower Color	Time of Bloom	Growth Habit	Hardiness	Growing Conditions
ABRONIA DESERT SAND VERBENA *Abronia villosa*	A sprawling, drought-tolerant annual from hot southwestern deserts. Sticky gray-green leaves contrast with showy clusters of bright pink, fragrant, 1/3-in. flowers that often persist over a month.	●	Winter to late spring	Height: 3–6" Spread: 1–2'	Tender annual	Full sun. Well-drained, sandy soil. In zones 9–11 sow seeds 1/4 in. deep in fall. Elsewhere start seedlings indoors in late winter and transplant after danger of frost has passed. Abronia is good for ground covers and coastal gardens.
ACHILLEA YARROW *Achillea millefolium*	A perennial with fernlike, gray-green, 1- to 2-in.-long leaves that are aromatic when touched. Leafy stems bear flat-topped clusters of white flowers and make long-lasting additions to fresh arrangements.	○	Late spring to late summer	Height: 1½–3½' Spread: 8–12"	3 to 10	Full sun to partial shade. Moderately rich, well-drained soil. Plants tolerate hot, dry conditions; over-watering may cause mildew. Yarrow may spread rapidly; divide it periodically. It is excellent in borders or meadows.
ACORUS SWEET FLAG *Acorus americanus*	A wetland perennial of the arum family whose 2- to 4-ft., swordlike leaves each have a single rib. Both the leaves and the 1- to 3-in., coblike cluster of yellow-green flowers are fragrant.	●	Late spring to late summer	Height: 3–6' Spread: 1–2'	4 to 11	Full sun to partial shade. Sweet flag grows best in waterlogged or wet soil in shallow ponds, but it adapts to upland soils, except those that dry out completely. Plants may benefit from dividing the rhizomes every several years.
ACTAEA WHITE BANEBERRY *Actaea pachypoda* RED BANEBERRY ◀ *A. rubra*	Native eastern perennials with cylindrical clusters of thin-petaled white flowers and deep green leaves with toothed leaflets. A. pachypoda has white berries on pink stalks; A. rubra, red ones on green stalks. The berries are poisonous.	○	Mid-spring	Height: 1–2½' Spread: 1–2'	3 to 7	Partial to full shade. Moist, well-drained, humus-rich soil. Baneberry does well in woodland conditions. It needs constant moisture but dislikes very wet soil. Divide roots in spring.
ALLIUM NODDING ONION, WILD ONION *Allium cernuum*	A midwestern perennial with umbels of fragrant, light pink, 1/3-in. flowers that bend toward the ground. The soft, grasslike leaves and 1- to 2-ft. flower stalks emerge from tiny, elongated bulbs.	○ ●	Midsummer	Height: 6–24" Spread: 4–6"	4 to 8	Full sun to partial shade. Moist, humus-rich soil. Plants will grow in damp soil but not soil that dries out completely. Wild onion is easy to grow in gardens or in meadows where grasses are not thick.

◀ *Indicates species shown*

Wildflowers & Native Plants

		Flower Color	Time of Bloom	Growth Habit	Hardiness	Growing Conditions
AMSONIA BLUESTAR *Amsonia tabernaemontana*	A perennial bearing dense clusters of light blue, ½-in., trumpet-shaped flowers with 5 long, pointed petals. The flowers bloom on somewhat shrubby stems that arise in clumps. The willowlike leaves of this perennial turn golden yellow in autumn.	●	Mid-spring to early summer	Height: 1½–3' Spread: 2–3'	3 to 9	Partial sun to shade. Evenly moist, well-drained, humus-rich soil. Bluestar is easy to grow, as long as the soil is not allowed to dry out. Trim shoots back to 1 ft. after flowering, unless you want to use pods in flower arrangements.
ANEMONE CANADA ANEMONE ◀ *Anemone canadensis* PASQUEFLOWER *A. patens*	Meadow and prairie perennials with attractive 2-in. flowers. Taller *A. canadensis* has white flowers and smooth, deep green leaves. *A. patens* blooms in early spring with white, lavender, or blue flowers followed by fuzzy leaves.	○ ● ●	A. canad. Mid-spring to early summer A. patens Late winter to early spring	A. canad. Height: 1–2' Spread: 1–2" A. patens Height: 4–8" Spread: 4–8"	A. canad. 2 to 6 A. patens 1 to 7	Full sun to partial shade. Well-drained, evenly moist soil. *A. canadensis* grows well in humus-rich soil; *A. patens* grows best in sandy loam. *A. canadensis* can become weedy in garden beds but spreads less in grassy meadows.
ANEMONELLA RUE ANEMONE *Anemonella thalictroides*	A perennial native to the eastern woodlands that strongly resembles a small anemone. Several dainty 1-in. flowers with pink or white petal-like sepals are borne on slender stalks above whorls of 3-lobed leaves.	○	Early to mid-spring	Height: 4–8" Spread: 2–4"	3 to 9	Partial to full shade. Moist, well-drained, humus-rich soil. Rue anemones need constant moisture but dislike very wet soil.
ANTENNARIA EVERLASTING, PUSSYTOES *Antennaria parvifolia*	A creeping perennial of the Great Plains and Southwest whose short flower stems rise above rosettes of spatula-shaped, woolly, gray-green, 1-in. leaves. The tiny, ¼-in., white flower heads are long-lasting.	○	Late spring to late summer	Height: 2–6" Spread: 2–6"	4 to 7	Full sun. Well-drained, sandy, rocky, or gravelly soil. Plants are drought resistant once established. With time, everlasting spreads by underground stolons.
AQUILEGIA COLORADO COLUMBINE *Aquilegia caerulea* COMMON COLUMBINE, EASTERN COLUMBINE ◀ *A. canadensis*	Perennials bearing attractive blue-green leaves with rounded leaflets. *A. caerulea* has blue-and-white flowers; *A. canadensis* has red-and-yellow ones. Each flower has 5 tubular petals ending in knob-tipped spurs.	● ●	A. caer. Early to mid-summer A. canad. Mid- to late spring	A. caer. Height: 1–2½' Spread: 9–18" A. canad. Height: 1–3' Spread: 9–18"	A. caer. 2 to 7 A. canad. 3 to 8	Full sun to partial shade. Well-drained, humus-rich soil. Both species are easy to grow from seed. Remove leaves showing leaf-miner tunnels or stems showing borer damage. *A. canadensis* can be grown as a rock garden or meadow plant.

		Flower Color	Time of Bloom	Growth Habit	Hardiness	Growing Conditions
ARGEMONE PRICKLY POPPY *Argemone hispida*	A perennial with spiny, light blue-green stems and foliage that emit a sticky yellow sap when injured. Clusters of prickly flower buds are borne atop stems and open into 2- to 4-in., 6-petaled flowers that have the texture of crepe paper.	○	Summer	Height: 1–2' Spread: 6–12"	4 to 9	Full sun. Well-drained, sandy, gravelly soil. Plants adapt to most soils, except those that are constantly moist, and may become weedy in optimal conditions. Prickly poppy can be grown as an annual.
ARISAEMA GREEN-DRAGON *Arisaema dracontium* JACK-IN-THE-PULPIT ◀ *A. triphyllum*	Perennials whose tiny flowers are clustered together on a column surrounded by a leafy bract called a spathe. A. dracontium has a green spathe with a narrow tip; the purple-striped spathe of A. triphyllum is broader.	● ●	Mid-spring to early summer	A. drac. Height: 1½–3' Spread: 1–2' A. triph. Height: 6–24" Spread: 6–15"	A. drac. 5 to 9 A. triph. 3 to 8	Partial sun to full shade. Humus-rich, moist soil. Both species tolerate a range of soil conditions, from well-drained and evenly moist to wet and nearly waterlogged. Arisaema is easily grown from seeds, which are contained in the bright red fruits.
ARUNCUS GOATSBEARD *Aruncus dioicus*	An eastern woodland perennial with dense, dark green, compound leaves. Both the male and female plants bear plumes of creamy white, fragrant, ⅛-in. flowers.	○	Mid- to late spring	Height: 4–7' Spread: 2–4'	4 to 9	Full sun to shade. Humus-rich, evenly moist soil that never completely dries out. Divide clumps every several years in early spring.
ASARUM WILD GINGER ◀ *Asarum canadense* *A. shuttleworthii*	Woodland perennials with rootstocks that smell and taste like ginger. The heart-shaped leaves arch over to hide 3-part, ½- to 1-in., thimble-shaped maroon flowers. A. shuttleworthii is evergreen and A. canadense is deciduous.	●	Spring to early summer	Height: 6–9" Spread: 6–12"	A. canad. 3 to 7 A. shut. 6 to 8	Partial to full shade. Moist, loamy soil that never completely dries out. Asarum is easy to grow and will spread with time. Creeping rootstocks can be easily divided.
ASCLEPIAS SWAMP MILKWEED *Asclepias incarnata* COMMON MILKWEED ◀ *A. syriaca*	Perennials with milky sap in their leaves and stems. Their rough pods release seeds with silky white hairs. A. incarnata has clusters of small, fragrant purple flowers. A. syriaca has clusters of greenish to rosy purple flowers.	● ●	Midsummer	A. incarn. Height: 4–5' Spread: 1–1½' A. syr. Height: 3–6' Spread: 1–1½'	A. incarn. 4 to 9 A. syr. 3 to 8	Full sun. A. incarnata: moist to wet soil or bog conditions. A. syriaca: moist, well-drained soil of average fertility. This species grows well in fields and dry meadows and spreads rapidly through rootstocks.

◀ *Indicates species shown*

Wildflowers & Native Plants

			Flower Color	Time of Bloom	Growth Habit	Hardiness	Growing Conditions
	ASCLEPIAS BUTTERFLY WEED *Asclepias tuberosa*	A perennial bearing flat-topped umbels of ornate ⅓-in. flowers with fused petals. A. tuberosa has orange flowers and fuzzy leaves scattered along the stems.	● ● ●	Summer	Height: 1–3' Spread: 6–12"	3 to 10	Full sun. Well-drained, evenly moist soil. Once established, butterfly weed is quite drought tolerant. It tends to rot if the soil remains wet during winter. Plants are easy to grow from plumed seeds.
	ASTER BLUE WOOD ASTER, HEART-LEAVED ASTER ◄ *Aster cordifolius* SMOOTH ASTER *A. laevis*	Blue-flowered perennial asters native to eastern woodlands and openings. Flowers are ½ to ¾ in. wide. A. cordifolius has toothed, heart-shaped leaves. A. laevis has elongated, toothless leaves that clasp whitish stems.	●	Late summer to mid-autumn	A. cord. Height: 1–5' Spread: 6–12" A. laevis Height: 1–3' Spread: 6–12"	3 to 8	Full sun to light shade. Humus-rich, evenly moist, well-drained soil. Once established, these asters are relatively drought resistant.
	ASTER NEW ENGLAND ASTER ◄ *Aster novae-angliae* NEW YORK ASTER *A. novi-belgii*	Tall, hardy perennials whose 1- to 2-in. ray flowers have bright gold centers. New England aster has larger, bright purple flowers, while those of New York aster are smaller and light blue.	● ●	Late summer to late autumn	A. n.-a. Height: 1–6' Spread: 1–2' A. n.-b. Height: 1–4½' Spread: 1–2'	A. n.-a. 3 to 7 A. n.-b. 4 to 8	Full sun to light shade. Humus-rich, evenly moist soil. Leaves are susceptible to powdery mildew. Divide mature clumps every 3 or 4 years. These asters are excellent meadow and prairie plants.
	BAILEYA DESERT MARIGOLD *Baileya multiradiata*	A woolly-leaved perennial of southwestern deserts. The 1- to 2-in., bright yellow, daisylike flowers have blunt outer petals and large, brilliant yellow centers. The flower heads, borne singly on hairy stems, turn white as they go to seed.		Spring to autumn	Height: 1–1½' Spread: 6–12"	7 to 11 (Grow as a half-hardy annual elsewhere)	Full sun. Well-drained, sandy soil. Extra moisture will prolong flowering season, but too much will lead to root rot. Baileya is an excellent rock garden plant that requires little attention.
	BAPTISIA BLUE FALSE INDIGO ◄ *Baptisia australis* YELLOW FALSE INDIGO *B. tinctoria*	Perennials with spikes of pealike flowers and gray-green foliage. Dark legume pods persist into winter. The 1-in. indigo flowers of B. australis are borne on stout branches, while the ½-in. yellow flowers of B. tinctoria are borne on thin branches.	●	Late spring to late summer	B. aust. Height: 2–6' Spread: 1–3' B. tinc. Height: 1–3' Spread: 1–2'	B. aust. 3 to 8 B. tinc. 5 to 10	Full sun to partial shade. Well-drained, evenly moist, slightly acid soil. These false indigos do not tolerate soggy soil conditions.

	Flower Color	Time of Bloom	Growth Habit	Hardiness	Growing Conditions
BIDENS TICKSEED, TICKSEED SUNFLOWER *Bidens aristosa* A tall perennial with deeply divided, toothed leaves and showy, bright yellow, 2- to 3-in. ray flowers. The small (1/3-in.), flat seeds have a pair of bristled horns. Tickseed is an attractive member of the sunflower family.		Late summer to late autumn	Height: 3–4' Spread: 1–2'	4 to 8	Full sun to light shade. Moist or wet, humus-rich soil that never completely dries out. Tickseed is a native of wet and open swampy places in the Midwest and East.
BOLTONIA BOLTONIA *Boltonia asteroides* An easy-to-grow perennial with masses of 1-in., aster-like white, pink, or lilac-purple flowers with yellow centers. The linear, 1- to 4-in. leaves are an attractive gray green.	○ ● ●	Late summer to late autumn	Height: 4–6' Spread: 3–5'	3 to 9	Full sun to partial shade. Well-drained, evenly moist soil that never completely dries out. Divide mature clumps every several years to keep plants from becoming too large and leggy.
BRODIAEA WILD HYACINTH ◀ *Brodiaea hyacinthina* *(Triteleia hyacinthina)* BLUE-DICKS *B. pulchella* *(Dichelostemma pulchellum)* Perennial bulbs native to the Pacific Coast with grass-like leaves and clusters of 1/2-in., hyacinth-like flowers atop leafless stems. The white flowers of B. hyacinthina appear in open umbels; the purple or blue flowers of B. pulchella form a dense head.	○ ● ●	B. hyac. Late spring to late summer B. pul. Spring	Height: 1–2½' Spread: 4–8"	B. hyac. 8 to 10 B. pul. 9 to 10	Full sun to light shade. B. hyacinthina: moist, humus-rich soil that never completely dries out. B. pulchella: well-drained soil that dries out only after flowering has finished.
CALLA WATER ARUM, WILD CALLA *Calla palustris* A wetland perennial resembling a small florist's calla. A 2-in., white spathe surrounds a club-like cluster of tiny golden flowers at the center. Heart-shaped, 6-in. leaves are borne on long, 10-in. stems.	○	Late spring to late summer	Height: 6–18" Spread: 6–18"	3 to 6	Full sun to partial shade. Constantly moist or even wet soil that is rich in humus. Wild callas grow well in standing water, making them ideal plants for water, bog, and poolside gardens.
CALLIRHOE WINECUP *Callirhoe Involucrata* A sprawling perennial native to the Great Plains with many chalice-shaped, 1- to 2-in., hollyhock-like flowers that have rose-purple petals with a white splotch at their bases. The hairy, dark green leaves have 5 to 7 lobes.	● ●	Early spring to early summer	Height: 6–36" Spread: 1–3'	4 to 8	Full sun. Well-drained, slightly acid soil. Plants are drought resistant. Prolong the flowering season by removing flowers as they fade. Callirhoe is excellent for rock gardens or sunny banks, or as a ground cover.

◀ *Indicates species shown*

Wildflowers & Native Plants

		Flower Color	Time of Bloom	Growth Habit	Hardiness	Growing Conditions
CALOCHORTUS PURPLE GLOBE TULIP *Calochortus amoenus* YELLOW MARIPOSA ◄ *C. luteus*	Western natives with grass-like leaves. Long, thin, erect stems carry attractive flowers with darker blotches at the bases of their 3 petals. C. amoenus has ½-in., drooping pink flowers; those of C. luteus are upright, 2 to 3 in., and deep yellow.	○ ◐	Late spring to early summer	C. amoe. Height: 6–20" Spread: 4–6" C. lut. Height: ½–2½' Spread: 4–6"	8 to 9	C. amoenus: *light shade. Evenly moist, well-drained soil.* C. luteus: *full sun. Well-drained, dry soil.* C. luteus *is drought tolerant.*
CALTHA MARSH MARIGOLD *Caltha palustris*	A slow-growing perennial with rich yellow flowers that resemble 1½-in. buttercups and are borne just above bright green, rounded leaves. After flowers produce fruits, the plants die back to their underground rhizomes.		Spring	Height: 1–2' Spread: 1–1½'	2 to 8	*Full sun to partial shade. Constantly moist, damp, or wet soil. Marsh marigolds are ideal plants for wetland, streamside, or bog gardens.*
CAMASSIA LEICHTLIN CAMASS ◄ *Camassia leichtlinii* COMMON CAMASS *C. quamash*	Perennial Pacific Coast bulbs that produce racemes of blue or white, star-shaped, 6-part flowers among clumps of grasslike foliage. The flowers' petal-like segments twist together after pollination.	○ ◐ ● ●	Spring to early summer	C. leicht. Height: 2–4' Spread: 6–12" C. quam. Height: 1–2½' Spread: 4–8"	5 to 9	*Full sun. Moist soil that dries out only after flowering has finished. Native to wet mountain meadows,* Camassia *can be grown at lower elevations if sufficient moisture is provided.*
CAMPANULA SOUTHERN HAREBELL *Campanula divaricata* BLUEBELLS OF SCOTLAND ◄ *C. rotundifolia*	Perennials with 5-lobed, bell-like, ¾-in. flowers that are usually pale blue but may be white, lavender, or violet blue. C. divaricata, native to southeastern woodlands, has 1-in., lance-like leaves; C. rotundifolia has 3-in., grasslike leaves.	◐	Late spring to early autumn	C. divar. Height: 1–3' Spread: 6–12" C. rotun. Height: 6–18" Spread: 4–8"	C. divar. 6 to 9 C. rotun. 2 to 9	C. divaricata: *Light shade; well-drained, rocky soil that is low in fertility.* C. rotundifolia: *Full sun to light shade; well-drained, sandy or gravelly soil.* C. rotundifolia *is a good plant for rock gardens or sandy meadows.*
CASTILLEJA INDIAN-PAINTBRUSH *Castilleja coccinea* PURPLE PAINTBRUSH ◄ *C. purpurea*	Native prairie plants with small flowers surrounded by fan-shaped bracts that resemble paint-dipped brushes. C. coccinea has red-tipped bracts; C. purpurea has purple-tipped bracts.	◐ ● ● ●	C. cocc. Mid-spring to late summer C. purp. Spring	C. cocc. Height: 6–24" Spread: 4–8" C. purp. Height: 6–12" Spread: 2–4"	C. cocc. 3 to 9 C. purp. 6 to 9	*Full sun to very light shade.* C. coccinea: *moist, peaty, gravelly soil or damp sand rich in humus.* C. purpurea: *alkaline, dryish soil. These plants do best in meadows where their roots can parasitize those of grasses.*

		Flower Color	Time of Bloom	Growth Habit	Hardiness	Growing Conditions
CHAMAELI-RIUM FAIRY-WAND *Chamaelirium luteum*	A native of damp eastern woodlands with separate male and female plants. Dense spikes of ¹/₈-in., white, 6-part flowers top long shoots above rosettes of spatula-shaped leaves. Males are smaller with creamier flowers.	○	Mid-spring to early summer	Height: 1–3' Spread: 6–12"	5 to 9	Filtered shade to full shade. Moist, humus-rich soil. Plants are good for natural-izing where soils are moist.
CHELIDONIUM CELANDINE *Chelidonium majus*	A Eurasian native that has become naturalized in the eastern U.S. Bright yellow, ³/₄-in., 4-petaled flowers are borne in small clusters on branched stems. The blue-green compound leaves emit an orange sap when broken.		Mid-spring to early summer	Height: 1–4' Spread: 6–12"	4 to 7	Full sun to partial shade. Evenly moist, well-drained, humus-rich soil. Celandine spreads rapidly and makes a good ground cover.
CHELONE TURTLEHEAD *Chelone glabra* PINK TURTLEHEAD ◄ *C. lyonii*	Native perennials whose spikes of 1-in., 2-lipped flowers resemble turtle heads. Pairs of 5-in. lance-shaped leaves clasp the light green stems. C. glabra has creamy white flowers; those of C. lyonii are bright pink.	○ ●	Late summer to early autumn	C. glabra Height: 1–6' Spread: 1–1¹/₂' C. lyonii Height: 1–3' Spread: 1–1¹/₂'	C. glabra 3 to 8 C. lyonii 5 to 9	Full sun to light shade. Humus-rich, moist soil that never completely dries out. Turtleheads are ideal plants for wetland and poolside gar-dens, but they will also tol-erate normal garden conditions. Both species spread freely with age.
CHIMAPHILA SPOTTED WINTERGREEN ◄ *Chimaphila maculata* COMMON PIPSISSEWA *C. umbellata*	Small woodland perennials with 2 whorls of leathery evergreen leaves and clusters of ¹/₂-in., waxy blossoms. C. maculata has white flowers and dark green leaves varie-gated with white. C. umbel-lata has pink flowers and uniformly green leaves.	○ ●	Summer	Height: 4–10" Spread: 4–8"	5 to 8	Full sun to partial shade. Well-drained, evenly moist, acid, humus-rich soil. Plants grow best in the filtered shade of oak woodlands.
CHRYSO-GONUM GREEN-AND-GOLD, GOLDEN STAR *Chrysogonum virginianum*	A long-blooming native perennial bearing single, bright gold composite flowers with pointed petals. Flowers are borne on short stems above a spreading, dense mat of lustrous green leaves.		Early spring to mid-summer	Height: 6–12" Spread: 6–12"	4 to 9	Full sun to medium shade, with some afternoon shade in warm climates. Well-drained but moist soil. Use a very thin mulch during winter in cooler climates, and remove it in early spring. Chrysogonum makes an excellent ground cover or bedding plant.

◄ *Indicates species shown*

Wildflowers & Native Plants

			Flower Color	Time of Bloom	Growth Habit	Hardiness	Growing Conditions
	CIMICIFUGA BLACK COHOSH, BLACK SNAKEROOT *Cimicifuga racemosa*	Bold, bushy perennial native to eastern woodlands. Wands of small (¹/₂-in.), creamy white, ill-scented flowers are borne atop long stems. The large, compound, light green leaves are deeply lobed.	○	Midsummer	Height: 3–8' Spread: 1–2'	3 to 8	Full sun to partial shade, with some afternoon shade in warm climates. Cimicifuga grows best in moist, well-drained, humus-rich soil that is not too acid. Plants grow slowly.
	CLARKIA FAREWELL-TO-SPRING, SATIN FLOWER *Clarkia amoena*	A Pacific Coast native that heralds the advent of summer with its showy, 2- to 4-in., 4-petaled flowers in pink, red, white, lavender, or combinations. The petals often have darker colors at their bases.	○ ● ● ●	Late spring to late summer	Height: 1–2¹/₂' Spread: 6–9"	Hardy annual	Full sun to light shade. Average, well-drained garden soil. Avoid fertilizing plants, or they will become leggy. Sow seeds in late autumn in zone 9 and warmer or in early spring elsewhere. Clarkia is drought tolerant once flowering starts.
	CLAYTONIA SPRING-BEAUTY *Claytonia virginica*	A dainty perennial native to eastern woodlands with delicate, 5-petaled, ¹/₂-in. flowers that are pink with darker pink stripes. Plants appear aboveground for only about a month in early spring, then die back to small underground tubers.	●	Early spring	Height: 4–12" Spread: 2–6"	4 to 8	Full sun to full shade. Humus-rich, evenly moist, well-drained soil. Spring-beauty does best when planted under deciduous trees and is excellent for naturalistic woodland gardens.
	CLINTONIA BLUEBEAD LILY *Clintonia borealis* SPECKLED WOOD LILY, WHITE CLINTONIA ◀ *C. umbellulata*	Native perennials whose leafless flower stalks bear umbels of bell-like flowers above clusters of 3 large, thick leaves. C. borealis has yellow flowers and blue fruits. C. umbellulata has white, brown-speckled flowers and black fruits.	○	Mid-spring to early summer	Height: 6–20" Spread: 4–8"	C. bor. 3 to 7 C. umbell. 5 to 7	Full sun to partial shade. Moist, humus-rich, acid soil. These plants prefer cool climates; they rarely succeed where average summer temperatures are much above 75°F.
	COLLINSIA CHINESE-HOUSES, INNOCENCE *Collinsia heterophylla*	An annual native to California with flowers that encircle the tops of the shoots in whorls. The ³/₄-in. flowers have blue-and-white upper lips, speckled with maroon, and purple lower lips. A velvety fuzz often covers the entire plant.	● ●	Mid-spring to early summer	Height: 1–2' Spread: 6–12"	Hardy annual	Dappled sun to shade; light shade is best, especially where summers are hot. Moist, well-drained, humus-rich soil. Deadhead withering flowers to prolong bloom. Collinsia is an excellent plant for shady borders, rock gardens, and cut flowers.

			Flower Color	Time of Bloom	Growth Habit	Hardiness	Growing Conditions
	COREOPSIS LANCE-LEAVED COREOPSIS *Coreopsis lanceolata* SEA DAHLIA ◀ *C. maritima*	These native perennials have bright golden, broad-petaled, daisylike flowers. C. lanceolata *has thin stems and lance-shaped leaves.* C. maritima *has fleshy stems and thin, dissected leaves.*		C. lanc. *Late spring to summer* C. mar. *Early spring to summer*	*C. lanc.* Height: 1–2½' Spread: 1–1½' *C. mar.* Height: 1–3' Spread: 1–2'	C. lanc. 4 to 9 C. mar. 9 to 11	Full sun. Well-drained, evenly moist, sandy soil. Both species are drought tolerant once established. C. maritima *is ideal for coastal gardens where winters are mild. The flowers are excellent for cutting.*
	CORNUS BUNCHBERRY *Cornus canadensis*	A perennial that is related to flowering dogwood but sprawls along the ground. Semiwoody stems carry 1- to 3-in. leaves in whorls. Small greenish white flowers, each surrounded by 4 white bracts, produce bright red, ¼-in. berries.	○	*Late spring*	Height: 4–9" Spread: 6–24"	2 to 6	Filtered sun to moderate shade. Moist, acid, peaty soil. In full sun the leaves are small and stunted. Bunchberry doesn't grow well in areas where summers are hot or dry.
	DARLING-TONIA COBRA LILY *Darlingtonia californica*	A perennial native to Pacific Northwest bogs with yellow-green, tubular, fluid-filled leaves that digest insects. The solitary 5-petaled, 3- to 4-in., light green flowers are tinged with purple and grow on separate shoots.	●	*Spring*	Height: 6–30" Spread: 6–18"	5 to 8	Filtered sun to partial shade. Wet, acid soil that is kept constantly moist. Provide plants with winter mulch in zone 7 and colder.
	DAUCUS WILD CARROT, QUEEN-ANNE'S-LACE *Daucus carota* var. *carota*	A biennial related to the carrot. Flower stems with ferny, light green leaves are each topped by a flat or slightly rounded, 4- to 6-in. cluster of tiny, creamy white, 5-petaled flowers. Some clusters have a single purple flower at the center.	◡	*Summer*	Height: 1–4' Spread: 6–18"	2 to 9	Full sun. Evenly moist, well-drained, sandy-loam, slightly acid soil. Queen-Anne's-lace is highly adaptable but tends to rot under soggy conditions. Plants can spread by seeds and become weedy with time.
	DELPHINIUM DWARF LARKSPUR *Delphinium menziesii* WILD LARKSPUR ◀ *D. tricorne*	Perennials that resemble cultivated larkspurs in having spurred flowers and deeply lobed leaves. D. menziesii *has rich blue flowers and hairy leaves and stems.* D. tricorne *has blue, violet, or variegated flowers and smooth leaves.*	●	D. menz. *Mid-spring to early summer* D. tri. *Mid- to late spring*	*D. menz.* Height: 6–24" Spread: 6–12" *D. tri.* Height: 1–3' Spread: 6–12"	D. menz. 6 to 9 D. tri. 4 to 8	Full sun to partial shade. Well-drained, evenly moist, humus-rich soil. D. menziesii *is native to the Pacific Northwest woodlands, D. tricorne to woodlands in the East.*

◀ *Indicates species shown*

Wildflowers & Native Plants

		Flower Color	Time of Bloom	Growth Habit	Hardiness	Growing Conditions
DICENTRA DUTCHMAN'S-BREECHES ◄ *Dicentra cucullaria* WILD BLEEDING-HEART *D. eximia*	Eastern woodland perennials with ferny foliage and fleshy stalks that bear intricate ½-in. flowers. D. cucullaria *has rows of spurred, white, fragrant flowers that look like upside-down trousers. D. eximia has pink flowers that look like elongated hearts.*	○ ●	D. cucul. *Early to mid-spring* D. exim. *Late spring to autumn*	D. cucul. Height: 6–12" Spread: 6–12" D. exim. Height: 1–1½' Spread: 6–12"	D. cucul. 3 to 7 D. exim. 3 to 9	Full sun to full shade. Moist, well-drained, alkaline to slightly acid (pH 6–8) soil. Dicentra *occurs naturally in rich woodland soil.*
DIONAEA VENUS'S-FLYTRAP *Dionaea muscipula*	An insect-eating perennial native to Carolina bogs. The reddish leaves have sensor hairs that trigger movements fast enough to trap insects. A flower shoot bearing small, white, 5-petaled flowers emerges from the rosette of leaves.	○	Spring	Height: 3–15" Spread: 3–10"	8 to 9	Partial sun. Damp, acid soil. High humidity is essential for growing Venus's-flytrap.
DODECA-THEON SHOOTING-STAR *Dodecatheon clevelandii* ◄ *D. meadia*	Perennials bearing clusters of small cyclamen-like flowers, each with 5 reflexed petals. The western D. clevelandii *is rose. D. meadia, an eastern native, is usually white, but may be pink. Plants die back to rootstocks in summer.*	○ ●	Spring	Height: 8–18" Spread: 8–18"	D. clev. 8 to 11 D. mead. 3 to 8	Full sun to shade. Humus-rich, well-drained soil that is moist during the flowering season. When they are dormant, plants can tolerate drier soil conditions.
DROSERA ROUND-LEAVED SUNDEW *Drosera rotundifolia*	A perennial that catches insects that land on the glistening, sticky glands covering the ¾- to 2-in. leaves. A shoot bearing tiny, white, 5-petaled flowers emerges from the rosette of small, ½- to 2-in.-long leaves.	○	Summer	Height: 2–12" Spread: 2–4"	3 to 9	Full sun to partial shade. Damp, acid soil. Sundews thrive under bog conditions or where sandy soil remains constantly moist.
ECHINACEA PALE CONEFLOWER *Echinacea pallida* PURPLE CONEFLOWER ◄ *E. purpurea*	Sturdy prairie natives bearing large daisylike blooms with dusky pink outer petals and domed, spiny centers of iridescent golden bronze florets. E. pallida *has thinner and paler pink outer petals that droop more than those of* E. purpurea.	●	E. pall. *Late spring to early summer* E. purp. *Summer to autumn*	Height: 2–4' Spread: 1–2'	3 to 8	Full sun to light shade. Well-drained, sandy-loam soil. Echinacea *is relatively drought tolerant and very easy to grow. Both species make ideal meadow plants.*

			Flower Color	Time of Bloom	Growth Habit	Hardiness	Growing Conditions
	EPILOBIUM FIREWEED *Epilobium angustifolium*	A North American perennial that quickly appears following forest fires. Tall wands of lovely rose pink blossoms contain clusters of up to 100-inch-wide, 4-petaled flowers. Flowering starts at the bottom and progresses upward.	●	*Summer*	Height: 2–7' Spread: 6–12"	2 to 9	*Full sun. Moist or even damp, bare, mineral-rich soil. Once established, fireweed can tolerate fairly dry soil. Grow from seed or propagate from divisions of underground rhizomes.*
	ERIGERON BEACH ASTER ◄ *Erigeron glaucus* PHILADELPHIA FLEABANE *E. philadelphicus*	Perennials with flowers that resemble daisies with thin, ragged outer petals. E. glaucus is sprawling and somewhat succulent with 2-in. lilac flowers. E. philadelphicus is erect with 3/4-in. white to deep pink flowers.	● ●	*Mid-spring to late summer*	E. glau. Height: 4–20" Spread: 1–2' E. phil. Height: 6–30" Spread: 6–18"	E. glau. 8 to 11 E. phil. 4 to 9	*Full sun. Evenly moist, well-drained soil. Both species grow best where the soil never completely dries out.*
	ERYNGIUM RATTLESNAKE-MASTER *Eryngium yuccifolium*	A prairie native with tough, fibrous, light green, yucca-like leaves that have spiny edges. Tiny greenish white flowers are clustered into globular, 3/4- to 1-in. heads. The fragrant flowers attract bees.	○	*Early to mid-summer*	Height: 1–6' Spread: 1–3'	4 to 9	*Full sun to very light shade. Well-drained, evenly moist soil. Once established, Eryngium tolerates drought. Protect young plants from being eaten by deer and rabbits.*
	ERYTHRONIUM EASTERN TROUT LILY ◄ *Erythronium americanum* AVALANCHE LILY *E. montanum*	Perennials with pairs of leaves from which a stalk arises bearing 6-part, nodding flowers. E. americanum has solitary bright yellow flowers and mottled leaves. E. montanum has several white flowers per stalk.	○	*E. amer.* *Early to mid-spring* *E. mont.* *Spring*	E. amer. Height: 3–10" Spread: 2–6" E. mont. Height: 6–12" Spread: 4–8"	E. amer. 3 to 9 E. mont. 5 to 8	*Full sun to shade. Well-drained, evenly moist, humus-rich soil; sites under deciduous trees are ideal. E. americanum is native to eastern woodlands; E. montanum, to Pacific Coast alpine meadows.*
	ESCHSCHOLZIA CALIFORNIA POPPY *Eschscholzia californica*	A short-lived perennial native to California. Poppy-like, 1- to 3-in., 4-petaled, fragrant, cupped flowers contrast with the gray-green ferny foliage. Flower color varies from pale yellow to deep orange.	●	*Early spring to autumn*	Height: 1–2' Spread: 6–12"	9 to 11 (Grow as an annual elsewhere)	*Full sun. Well-drained soil of average fertility. Eschscholzia, an easily grown, highly adaptable species, is excellent for naturalizing on sunny hillsides.*

◄ *Indicates species shown*

Wildflowers & Native Plants

		Flower Color	Time of Bloom	Growth Habit	Hardiness	Growing Conditions
EUPATORIUM HARDY AGERATUM, MIST FLOWER *Eupatorium coelestinum* JOE-PYE WEED ◀ *E. purpureum*	Perennials with flat-topped clusters of fuzzy flowers. E. coelestinum *has powder blue flowers and pairs of triangular leaves.* E. pur- pureum *has pink-purple flowers and whorls of lance-shaped leaves.*	● ● ●	Late summer to mid- autumn	E. coel. Height: 1–3' Spread: 6–18" E. purp. Height: 2–10' Spread: 1–3'	E. coel. 6 to 11 E. purp. 4 to 9	Full sun to light shade. E. coelestinum *prefers well-drained, sandy soil; under ideal circumstances it may become weedy.* E. pur- pureum *requires moist, humus-rich soil that does not dry out completely.*
FILIPENDULA QUEEN-OF-THE- PRAIRIE *Filipendula rubra*	A perennial native to moist prairies and bearing beau- tiful foamy clusters of tiny, light pink, 5-petaled flowers atop long stems. Leaves are big (up to 3 ft.), angular, and cut into 7 to 9 pointed lobes.	●	Summer	Height: 2–8' Spread: 1–2'	3 to 9	Full sun to light shade. Evenly moist, well-drained soil that is rich in organic matter. Filipendula *will thrive even in wet soil and is an ideal plant for wet meadows.*
FRAGARIA WILD STRAWBERRY *Fragaria virginiana*	A creeping meadow peren- nial with compound leaves that have 3 toothed leaflets. The ½-in., roselike flowers have white petals and gold centers. Seedlike fruits are embedded in a small (³/₁₆- to ¾-in.) edible berry, which is part of the flower.	○	Mid- to late spring	Height: 3–6" Spread: 3–6"	3 to 7	Full sun to partial shade. Well-drained, evenly moist, humus-rich, acid soil. F. vir- giniana, *with its wonderfully flavored berries, is one of the wild species from which hybrid strawberries have been developed.*
GAILLARDIA BLANKET FLOWER *Gaillardia pulchella*	An annual with daisylike, 2- to 3-in., dark red flowers with yellow tips and purple- red centers. Varied colors are available in other naturally occurring forms of the plant.	●	Summer	Height: 1–2' Spread: 6–12"	Hardy annual	Full sun. Dry to average soil. In zone 8 and warmer, sow seeds where desired in winter; elsewhere sow seeds in early spring or start indoors 6 weeks before last frost. Gaillardia *is easy to grow.*
GALAX COLTSFOOT *Galax urceolata (G. aphylla)*	An evergreen perennial native to the woods of the southern Appalachians. Long spikes of tiny white flowers are borne above lustrous, rounded, 5-in. leaves that turn bronze in autumn.	○	Early to mid- summer	Height: 1–1½' Spread: 6–18"	6 to 8	Filtered sun to full shade. Evenly moist, well-drained, humus-rich, acid soil. Galax spreads slowly with age and makes an ideal ground cover.

			Flower Color	Time of Bloom	Growth Habit	Hardiness	Growing Conditions
	GAULTHERIA WINTERGREEN, TEABERRY *Gaultheria procumbens*	A low, evergreen north-eastern native perennial with white, 1/2-in., urn-shaped flowers producing 1/4-in. red berries that last into winter. Wintergreen-flavored leaves are bright green when young but become leathery and reddish in fall.	○	Summer	Height: 2–4" Spread: 4–12"	3 to 8	Filtered sun to full shade, but grows best in sunny patches. Dry or wet, acid, humus-rich soil. Wintergreen tolerates a wide variety of moisture conditions, from boggy to dry and sandy, and makes a good ground cover.
	GENTIANA BOTTLE GENTIAN, CLOSED GENTIAN *Gentiana andrewsii*	A perennial with deep blue flowers borne in whorled clusters near the tips of branched stems. Bumblebees pollinate the flowers by forcing their way into the tightly closed petals. Reddish stems are clasped by pairs of 2- to 4-in. leaves.	●	Late summer to early autumn	Height: 1–3' Spread: 1–2'	3 to 9	Full sun to partial shade. Moist soil. Plants thrive where soil is soggy; ideal for planting along streamsides and in wet meadows. Propagate by division in spring or sow seeds in fall; divide and replant every 3 years in fresh soil.
	GERANIUM WILD GERANIUM *Geranium maculatum*	An eastern woodland and meadow native with clusters of lavender-pink, 1-in., 5-petaled flowers that produce intriguing 5-part, dark brown, beaked fruits by summer. Attractive dark green leaves have 5 deep lobes.	◐ ◐	Mid-spring to early summer	Height: 1–2' Spread: 1–3'	4 to 7	Full sun to partial shade. Evenly moist, well-drained, humus-rich soil. Wild geranium grows best in light shade in soil that never completely dries out. Plants spread slowly with age, forming a ground cover with beautiful flowers.
	GEUM PRAIRIE SMOKE *Geum triflorum*	A native prairie perennial with numerous 4- to 9-in., ferny, blue-green leaves in clumps from which shoots bearing 3 flowers arise. Each flower has 5 rosy petals and sepals. Fruits with wispy gray "tails" give Geum its common name	● ●	Mid- to late spring	Height: 6–18" Spread: 6–12"	2 to 5	Full sun to light shade. Evenly moist, well-drained soil. Geum is an ideal rock garden plant. It grows well in meadows, as long as grasses are not too thick.
	GILIA QUEEN-ANNE'S-THIMBLE *Gilia capitata* STANDING CYPRESS ◀ *G. rubra* (*Ipomopsis rubra*)	Annuals and biennials with tubular, funnel-like, 5-lobed flowers and deeply dissected, feathery leaves. G. capitata has globular clusters of 1/2-in. blue or white flowers; G. rubra has up to 100 bright red, 1-in. flowers in a spikelike series.	○ ● ●	Summer	G. cap. Height: 1 1/2–3' Spread: 6–12" G. rubra Height: 2–6' Spread: 6–12"	G. cap. Hardy annual G. rubra 5 to 9 (Hardy biennial)	Full sun. Dry, well-drained soil. Sandy loam or even gravelly soil is best. Sow G. capitata in autumn in zone 9 and warmer; in spring elsewhere.

◀ *Indicates species shown*

Wildflowers & Native Plants

		Flower Color	Time of Bloom	Growth Habit	Hardiness	Growing Conditions
GILLENIA BOWMAN'S-ROOT, INDIAN-PHYSIC *Gillenia trifoliata*	Like many other members of the rose family, this native woodland perennial has showy flowers, each with 5 narrow white or pink petals surrounding a small cup of yellow stamens. The 3-part, toothed leaves appear to clasp the stem.	○ ●	Mid-spring to early summer	Height: 2–3' Spread: 1–2'	5 to 8	Filtered sun to partial shade. Well-drained, slightly acid, evenly moist soil. Native to the Midwest and Southeast, Gillenia *is an attractive plant for woodland gardens.*
HELENIUM SNEEZEWEED, YELLOW STAR *Helenium autumnale*	An eastern native perennial with showy yellow daisylike flowers with broad, toothed petals and domed centers atop branched stems. Leaf bases form "wings" that run down stems. Other naturally occurring forms have red, orange, or brown flowers.	● ●	Late summer to autumn	Height: 3–5' Spread: 6–18"	3 to 8	Full sun to light shade. Moist or wet soil. Plants benefit from being divided every several years. Helenium *is good for cutting.*
HELIANTHUS THIN-LEAF SUNFLOWER *Helianthus decapetalus*	A perennial related to the garden sunflower native to open woods, thickets, and woodland edges. The lance-shaped, 6- to 8-in. leaves have blades that form "wings" on the leafstalks. The 2- to 3-in.-wide yellow flowers have 10 outer petals.		Late summer to mid-autumn	Height: 2–5' Spread: 1–2'	4 to 8	Full sun to light shade. Well-drained, evenly moist soil. Helianthus *tolerates damp soil as well.*
HEPATICA LIVERLEAF, SHARP-LOBED HEPATICA *Hepatica acutiloba* ROUND-LOBED HEPATICA ◀ *H. americana*	Perennials with 1-in. white, pink, or blue flowers with 5 to 18 petals borne on hairy stems. H. acutiloba *has leaves with pointed lobes;* H. americana *has rounded lobes. Hepaticas are among the earliest spring flowers in eastern woodlands.*	○ ● ●	Early spring	Height: 3–6" Spread: 3–6"	3 to 7	Filtered sun to full shade. Evenly moist, well-drained, humus-rich soil; sites under deciduous trees are ideal. H. acutiloba *grows best in neutral to alkaline soil and benefits from additions of crushed limestone.* H. americana *requires acid soil.*
HESPERIS DAME'S ROCKET *Hesperis matronalis*	A native European biennial that has naturalized in U.S. deciduous forests and woodlands. The lavender, pink, or white $1/2$- to $3/4$-in. flowers each have 4 round-tipped petals. Leaves are dark green, toothed, and 3 to 4 in. long.	○ ● ●	Mid-spring	Height: 1–3' Spread: 6–12"	3 to 7	Full sun to full shade. Moist, humus-rich soil; sites under deciduous trees are ideal. Plants grow best in cool weather. Sow seeds in early spring for several successive years.

			Flower Color	Time of Bloom	Growth Habit	Hardiness	Growing Conditions
	HEUCHERA CORALBELLS *Heuchera sanguinea* ALUMROOT ◀ *H. villosa*	Perennials grown more for their mounds of foliage than their clusters of small, 5-petaled flowers. Semievergreen H. sanguinea has ¹⁄₃-in. reddish flowers and rounded leaves. Evergreen H. villosa has more triangular leaves and white flowers.	● ● ●	H. sang. *Late spring to summer* H. vill. *Midsummer to early autumn*	H. sang. Height: 1–2' Spread: 1–2' H. vill. Height: 2–3' Spread: 1–2'	H. sang. 4 to 8 H. vill. 5 to 9	Light shade. Well-drained, sandy, humus-rich soil. Heuchera is drought tolerant once established. Divide mature plants every 3 or 4 years. H. sanguinea is good in borders and rock gardens; H. villosa is an ideal ground cover for woodlands.
	HIBISCUS ROSE MALLOW ◀ *Hibiscus moscheutos* *H. palustris* (*H. moscheutos* subsp. *palustris*)	Large perennials native to North American coastal marshlands with 6- to 8-in., pink or white hollyhock-like flowers. The flowers of H. moscheutos have red centers; H. palustris has uniformly colored flowers.	○ ●	Late summer to early autumn	Height: 4–8' Spread: 2–4'	5 to 11	Full sun. Humus-rich, well-drained, moist soil. Both species benefit from winter mulching in zones 5–7. Japanese beetles, slugs, or rust disease may be a problem.
	HOUSTONIA BLUETS *Houstonia caerulea* (*Hedyotis caerulea*)	A short-lived perennial native to eastern meadows. It is most visible when its tiny (¹⁄₄- to ¹⁄₂-in.), 4-petaled, light blue, white, or violet flowers with yellow centers bloom in the spring; otherwise it blends in with grasses.	●	Mid- to late spring	Height: 2–8" Spread: 1–2"	4 to 8	Full sun to very light shade. Humus-rich, acid, moist soil. Bluets are excellent plants for wet meadows. If plants are naturalized in lawns, do not mow until after seeds have set in early summer.
	HYPERICUM ST.-JOHN'S-WORT *Hypericum perforatum*	A perennial with showy golden yellow, 1 in., 5-petaled flowers and pairs of 1- to 2-in., elliptical leaves with translucent dots. Flower petals have black dots on their margins. Flowers are said to begin blooming June 24, St. John's Day.		Early summer to early autumn	Height: 1–3' Spread: 1–3'	5 to 9	Full sun to light shade. Not choosy about soil conditions. Plants can become weedy where grasses are not thick and may be difficult to eradicate. St.-John's-wort is on the noxious weed list for several states in the West.
	HYPOXIS HAIRY STAR GRASS *Hypoxis hirsuta*	A perennial that is not really a grass but a small relative of the amaryllis. The grasslike, 1-ft. leaves are covered with downy fuzz. Clusters of several star-shaped, ¹⁄₂-in., bright yellow, 6-part flowers bloom at the tips of hairy stems.		Spring	Height: 3–6" Spread: 1–2"	5 to 9	Full sun to light shade. Well-drained, evenly moist soil. Plants do not tolerate constantly wet soil. Hypoxis is good for naturalizing in meadows or along woodland margins.

◀ *Indicates species shown*

Wildflowers & Native Plants

			Flower Color	Time of Bloom	Growth Habit	Hardiness	Growing Conditions
	IMPATIENS JEWELWEED, SPOTTED TOUCH-ME-NOT *Impatiens capensis*	An annual with tubular, ½- to 1-in., yellow-orange flowers speckled with red and suspended sideways on succulent stems. Torpedo-shaped green fruits explode when touched, shooting out seeds. Jewelweed is a favorite with hummingbirds.	●	Midsummer to autumn	Height: 1–5' Spread: 6–18"	Hardy annual	Full sun to full shade. Moist or wet, humus-rich soil; does not grow well in dry soil. Sow seeds in spring or autumn where plants are desired. Impatiens grows rapidly. Plants may become weedy but are easy to pull out.
	IRIS DWARF CRESTED IRIS *Iris cristata*	A perennial native to open woodlands with 2- to 3-in. violet-blue flowers borne on erect stems that arise amid flat, long leaves. This species of iris has single flowers on short, slender stems.	○ ◐ ●	Mid- to late spring	Height: 3–8" Spread: 2–6"	5 to 8	Partial shade. Well-drained, evenly moist, humus-rich soil. Plants spread with age.
	IRIS PACIFIC COAST IRIS *Iris douglasiana*	A Pacific Coast native with showy 3- to 4-in. flowers that bloom on sturdy stalks arising from clumps of 1- to 2-ft., sword-shaped leaves. The fragrant flowers are usually blue but also occur in pink, cream, or white.	○ ● ● ●	Spring	Height: 1–2' Spread: 6–12"	9 to 11	Partial shade to full sun. Evenly moist, well-drained, humus-rich, slightly acid soil; will not grow well in alkaline soil. Pacific Coast iris is an ideal perennial for rock gardens and shady banks but is difficult to grow in regions with cold winters.
	IRIS BLUE FLAG, WILD IRIS *Iris versicolor*	A native iris bearing narrow, flat, sword-shaped bluish green leaves up to 3 ft. long. The beardless flowers are usually blue-violet, but may be lavender, purple, red-violet, or white. Stems are straight or branched.	○ ● ●	Late spring to early summer	Height: 1–3' Spread: 6–12'	3 to 8	Full sun to partial shade. Moist to wet, humus-rich, slightly acid soil; sites by bogs or ponds are ideal. Blue flag will also grow in up to 6 in. of standing water. Plants self-sow. Propagate by division in early spring.
	JEFFERSONIA TWINLEAF *Jeffersonia diphylla*	An eastern woodland perennial whose 5- to 6-in.-wide leaves resemble light green butterflies with closed wings. Leafless flower stalks bear single, 1-in., 8-petaled white flowers with a mass of golden stamens.	○	Mid-spring	Height: 6–12" Spread: 4–8"	4 to 7	Partial to full shade. Evenly moist, well-drained, humus-rich, alkaline soil; sites under deciduous trees are ideal. Twinleaf does not tolerate dry soil.

		Flower Color	Time of Bloom	Growth Habit	Hardiness	Growing Conditions
LASTHENIA GOLDFIELDS *Lasthenia chrysostoma* *(Baeria chrysostoma)*	A meadow annual native to California with bright golden, ½- to 1-in., daisy-like flowers. Pairs of narrow, fuzzy leaves clasp the thin, reddish stems.		Spring	Height: 4–8" Spread: 4–8"	Tender annual	Full sun to light shade. Evenly moist, well-drained, humus-rich soil. Sow seeds in late autumn in zone 9 and warmer; in spring elsewhere. In warm regions Lasthenia self-seeds once established.
LAYIA TIDY-TIPS *Layia platyglossa*	A California grassland native bearing deep yellow, fragrant, 1- to 1½-in., daisylike flowers with long black anthers atop sprawling, hairy stems. The common name refers to the white tips on yellow ray petals encircling golden flower centers.	○	Spring to early summer	Height: 4–16" Spread: 2–8"	Tender annual	Full sun. Well-drained soil that is moist at least in early spring. In zone 9 and warmer, sow seeds outdoors in desired location in late fall to early spring. Elsewhere start seeds indoors 6 to 8 weeks before the last frost.
LEUCAN-THEMUM OXEYE DAISY *Leucanthemum vulgare* *(Chrysanthemum leucanthemum)*	A European perennial that has become naturalized in eastern U.S. fields. Atop thin, erect stems are 1- to 2-in. flower heads with white petals and golden centers. The bottom leaves are spatula shaped; those higher up are ferny.	○	Summer to early autumn	Height: 1–3' Spread: 6–18"	4 to 9	Full sun to light shade. Well-drained soil. Oxeye daisies are not choosy about soil conditions and can become weedy.
LEWISIA BITTER ROOT *Lewisia rediviva*	A western native with forked taproots that send up 1- to 3-in.-long, succulent leaves in late summer or autumn. The 2-in., many-petaled, pink or white flowers are borne in spring on stalks just above the rosettes of leaves.	○ ●	Early to mid-spring	Height: 4–6" Spread: 4–8"	3 to 10	Full sun. Well-drained, gravelly soil that dries out during the summer. Moderate water is needed during flowering season, but plants rot if soil is too moist while they are dormant. Lewisia is an ideal rock garden plant for dry climates.
LIATRIS PRAIRIE BLAZING STAR, THICK-SPIKE GAY-FEATHER *Liatris pycnostachya* SPIKE GAY-FEATHER ◀ *L. spicata*	Grassland perennials with small, rosy lavender flowers that bloom in shaggy clusters all along 1- to 2-ft. stems. The linear, grasslike leaves grow up to 1 ft. long at the base of the plant but are shorter at the bottom of the flower stems.	●	Midsummer to early autumn	L. pyc. Height: 2–5' Spread: 6–24" L. spic. Height: 1–3' Spread: 6–12"	3 to 9	Full sun to light shade. Well-drained, evenly moist, humus-rich soil. L. pycnostachya is more drought tolerant; L. spicata can be grown in wetter soil. Divide the corms of mature plants to keep them flowering vigorously.

◀ Indicates species shown

Wildflowers & Native Plants

		Flower Color	Time of Bloom	Growth Habit	Hardiness	Growing Conditions
LILIUM CANADA LILY *Lilium canadense*	A native perennial with nodding, 2- to 3-in., bell-shaped, 6-petaled flowers that grace wet places. The petals are light to dark orange with purple-flecked inner surfaces. Whorls of 4- to 6-in., lance-shaped leaves encircle 5-ft. stems.	●	Early to mid-summer	Height: 3–5' Spread: 6–12"	3 to 8	Full sun to light shade. Moist, humus-rich, acid soil that never completely dries out. Canada lily is ideal for wet meadows and boggy habitats. Deer like to eat the stems and flowers and may be a problem.
LILIUM WOOD LILY, FLAME LILY *Lilium philadelphicum*	A native perennial of both oak woodlands and prairies with 3- to 4-in., bright red-orange, purple-speckled flowers that point upward in groups of up to 5 per stem. Whorls of 3- to 4-in., lance-shaped leaves clasp the 3-ft. stems.	● ●	Early to mid-summer	Height: 8–36" Spread: 6–12"	4 to 7	Full sun to filtered shade. Well-drained, evenly moist, moderately acid, humus-rich soil. One of the most drought-tolerant lily species, wood lily grows well in relatively dry prairies and wood-land gaps.
LILIUM TURK'S-CAP LILY *Lilium superbum*	A bold wetland perennial native to moist meadows in the East. It has intensely orange petals that bend back sharply to reveal large brown anthers at the flower centers.	●	Mid- to late summer	Height: 5–8' Spread: 1–2'	5 to 8	Full sun to light shade. Moist, humus-rich soil that never completely dries out. Turk's-cap lily is ideal for both naturalistic gardens and formal borders. Deer like to eat stems and flowers and may be a problem.
LIMNANTHES MEADOW FOAM *Limnanthes douglasii*	A sprawling Pacific Coast native. Frothy, feathery, highly dissected leaves cover the ground beneath cupped, 1-in. flowers on long stalks. Each fragrant, bicolored flower has 5 notched petals with white tips and gold bases.	○	Late spring to mid-summer	Height: 4–12" Spread: 4–8"	Hardy annual	Full sun. Well-drained, evenly moist soil. Plant grows best in cool weather. Sow seeds outdoors in fall in zone 9 and warmer; in early spring elsewhere. Limnanthes is an excellent choice for moist meadows and rock gardens.
LINANTHUS LINANTHUS *Linanthus grandiflorus*	A striking native of the Pacific Coast with dense clusters of silky white, 1-in., trumpet-shaped flowers tinged with pink or lavender. Whorls of deeply cut, dark green leaves encircle the sprawling stems.	○ ●	Mid-spring to summer	Height: 4–20" Spread: 6–24"	Tender annual	Full sun in well-drained, evenly moist, sandy soil. In zone 9 and warmer, sow seeds outdoors in fall; else-where sow seeds outdoors in spring after soil is warm.

		Flower Color	Time of Bloom	Growth Habit	Hardiness	Growing Conditions
LOBELIA CARDINAL FLOWER ◀ *Lobelia cardinalis* GREAT BLUE LOBELIA *L. siphilitica*	Striking native perennials bearing 2-lipped flowers atop erect stems that emerge from rosettes of leaves. L. cardinalis *has 1½- to 2-in. bright red flowers pollinated by humming-birds.* L. siphilitica *has 1-in. light blue flowers.*	○ ◐ ● ●	Late summer to early autumn	L. card. Height: 1–5' Spread: 6–18" L. siph. Height: 1–3' Spread: 8–16"	L. card. 2 to 9 (Grow as an annual in colder regions) L. siph. 5 to 8	Full sun to full shade. Moist to wet, humus-rich soil. Lobelia *is not difficult to grow, but roots may be damaged by heaving from severe winter frosts. Reset roots in spring. Plants are ideal for shady streamsides.*
LUPINUS HARTWEG LUPINE *Lupinus hartwegii* TEXAS BLUEBONNET *L. texensis*	Annuals with clusters of pealike flowers atop stems bearing leaves with finger-like leaflets. L. hartwegii, *with blue-and-rose flowers, is popular in borders;* L. tex-ensis *has striking blue-and-white flowers that fill Texas grasslands with spring color.*	○ ◐ ●	L. hart. *Summer* L. tex. *Spring*	L. hart. Height: 2–3' Spread: 1–2' L. tex. Height: 6–18" Spread: 6–18"	L. hart. 9 to 11 (Grow as a hardy annual elsewhere) L. tex. Hardy annual	Full sun. Well-drained, average garden soil. Lupines respond well to additions of ground limestone. Sow seeds in spring after nicking the seed coat to speed germination.
LYSIMACHIA CREEPING JENNIE ◀ *Lysimachia nummularia* WHORLED LOOSE-STRIFE *L. quadrifolia*	Perennials with bright yel-low, ½-in., star-shaped flowers. L. nummularia *has single flowers above paired penny-sized leaves on trailing, rooted stems.* L. quadrifolia *has delicate flower stalks and whorls of 4 or 5 lance-shaped leaves.*		Summer	L. numm. Height: 1–2" Spread: 1–3' L. quad. Height: 1–2½' Spread: 4–8"	4 to 8	Full sun to partial shade. Humus-rich, evenly moist soil. L. nummularia *is easy to grow and can become inva-sive in humid regions.* L. quadrifolia *grows best in slightly acid, well-drained, evenly moist soil, although it tolerates moist soil as well.*
MENTZELIA BLAZING STAR *Mentzelia lindleyi*	A California native whose spectacular bright yellow, 5-petaled, 2- to 3-in. flowers open in the evening to reveal showers of golden stamens at their centers. The 2- to 3-in., hairy, dandelion-like leaves clasp the fuzzy stems.		Late spring to summer	Height: 1–4' Spread: 6–12"	Tender annual	Full sun. Average well-drained soil; sandy loam is ideal. Plants tolerate heat, drought, wind, and low fer-tility as long as drainage is sufficient. Sow seeds ⅛ in. deep in late autumn in zone 9 and warmer or in mid-spring elsewhere.
MERTENSIA VIRGINIA BLUEBELLS *Mertensia virginica*	A strikingly beautiful native of moist deciduous eastern woodlands. Sprays of deli-cate flowers are pink in bud, become powder blue in full flower, and fade to pink again with age. By mid-summer the top of the plant dies back and disappears.	◐	Mid- to late spring	Height: 1–2' Spread: 1–1½'	3 to 9	Full sun to partial shade. Mertensia *needs well-drained soil rich in organic matter and moist throughout the growing season. Plants will not tol-erate dry conditions and may be troubled by slugs and snails.*

◀ *Indicates species shown*

Wildflowers & Native Plants

		Flower Color	Time of Bloom	Growth Habit	Hardiness	Growing Conditions
MIMULUS BUSH MONKEY FLOWER *Mimulus aurantiacus*	A shrubby California native bearing pale to deep orange, 1- to 2-in., pouched flowers with white stigmatic surfaces that close quickly when touched. The stems and 2-in.-long leaves are covered with short, sticky hairs.	●	*Spring to summer*	Height: 1–4' Spread: 1–4'	9 to 11	*Full sun to light shade. Well-drained soil. Once established, this long-lived perennial is quite drought tolerant.*
MITCHELLA PARTRIDGEBERRY *Mitchella repens*	An eastern native ground cover effective in cool, shady sites, even under conifers. Pairs of round, dark green leaves with white veins line the sprawling stems. Trumpet-shaped white flowers produce red fruits.	○	*Late spring to early summer*	Height: 1–2" Spread: 1–2'	4 to 9	*Partial sun to full shade. Cool, moist, humus-rich, acid soil; sites among pines and hemlock are ideal. Partridge-berry can be grown indoors in containers year-round.*
MONARDA BEEBALM ◄ *Monarda didyma* WILD BERGAMOT *M. fistulosa*	Perennials bearing attractive clusters of bright red (M. didyma) or lavender (M. fistulosa), 2-lipped, tubular flowers. Pairs of lance-shaped leaves with a citrus scent clasp the slender, square stems.	○ ● ●	*Early to late summer*	Height: 2–4' Spread: 6–12"	4 to 8	*Full sun to partial shade. Evenly moist, well-drained, humus-rich soil. Monarda will tolerate very wet soil. Divide periodically to maintain vigor and keep in check. Plants are prone to mildew if allowed to become too crowded.*
NELUMBO AMERICAN LOTUS *Nelumbo lutea* (*N. pentapetala*)	A native aquatic perennial with 1- to 2-ft., bowl-shaped, blue-green leaves. Separate flower stalks bear showy, 4- to 8-in., pale yellow, many-petaled flowers with centers that resemble golden shower heads.		*Summer to early autumn*	Height: 3–7' Spread: 4–8'	4 to 8	*Full sun. Humus-rich soil submerged in water. Nelumbo requires considerable space and standing water.*
NEMOPHILA BABY-BLUE-EYES *Nemophila menziesii*	A fast-growing California native with many 1- to 1½-in., cupped flowers, each with 5 petals that have sky blue tips and white bases streaked with blue. The stems and soft, hairy leaves of this annual tend to sprawl along the ground.	●	*Late winter to mid-spring*	Height: 10–20" Spread: 6–12"	Hardy annual	*Full sun to partial shade. Well-drained, evenly moist soil that does not become wet while the plants are in flower. Plants are easy to grow from seed; sow seeds in fall in zones 9–11 and warmer and in early spring elsewhere.*

		Flower Color	Time of Bloom	Growth Habit	Hardiness	Growing Conditions

NYMPHAEA
FRAGRANT WATER LILY
Nymphaea odorata

One of the most attractive native aquatic plants. Stout, rooted rhizomes send up round, thick, 3- to 10-in. leaves and 3- to 5-in. white or pink, fragrant, many-petaled flowers that open in the morning and remain open for about 3 days.

○ ●

Summer to early autumn

Height: 6–12"

Spread: 1–5'

3 to 10

Full sun. Humus-rich soil submerged in water. Nymphaea requires standing water and is excellent for small aquatic gardens.

OENOTHERA
SUNDROPS
◀ *Oenothera fruticosa*
PINK EVENING PRIMROSE
O. speciosa

Native perennials with flowers that open during the day and close at night. O. fruticosa is more erect, with 1- to 2-in. bright yellow flowers. O. speciosa is sprawling, with light pink flowers that darken with age.

○ ●

O. frut. Late spring to early autumn

O. spec. Summer

O. frut. Height: 1–3' Spread: 6–12"

O. spec. Height: 1–2' Spread: 6–18"

O. frut. 4 to 7

O. spec. 5 to 9

Full sun to partial shade. Well-drained soil. O. fruticosa grows best in evenly moist, humus-rich soil. O. speciosa is more drought tolerant. It can become weedy but is easily uprooted.

OPUNTIA
PRICKLY PEAR
Opuntia humifusa

An eastern native cactus with flat, oval, 5-in. pads bearing prominent, stiff spines. The showy 3- to 4-in. flowers have many petals. The bulbous maroon fruits are edible, but watch out for small spines.

Late spring to early summer

Height: 1–2'

Spread: 1–1½'

4 to 10

Full sun. Well-drained, sandy or gravelly soil. Opuntia will not tolerate soggy conditions. Mulch during winter in zone 5, but don't let the pads rot. Plants may spread rapidly in sandy soil in warm climates.

ORTHOCARPUS
OWL'S-CLOVER
Orthocarpus copelandii
◀ *O. purpurascens*

Native Pacific Coast annuals with dense clusters of small magenta-and-yellow flowers nestled among pink, rose, and green bracts. O. copelandii has lance-shaped leaves; O. purpurascens has thin, somewhat ferny leaves.

● ●

O. cope. Late spring to summer

O. purp. Early to mid-spring

Height: 4–16"

Spread: 2–6"

Tender annuals

Full sun. O. copelandii: moist, humus-rich, cool soil, as in its native mountain meadows. O. purpurascens: well-drained, sandy soil, as in its native California grasslands.

OXALIS
WOOD SORREL
◀ *Oxalis acetosella*
O. montana

Low, creeping perennials of moist, shady woodlands with cloverlike leaves, each divided into 3 heart-shaped lobes. Delicate, 5-petaled, ⅓- to ½-in. flowers with white or pink, red-streaked petals bloom singly on slender stalks.

○ ●

Summer

Height: 2–5"

Spread: 6–18"

O. acet. 5 to 8

O. mont. 3 to 7

Filtered sun to shade. Cool, moist, humus-rich soil. O. montana, native to mountains of the East, grows best in acid soil where summers are cool. O. acetosella, a European native with slightly larger flowers, is not as hardy.

◀ *Indicates species shown*

Wildflowers & Native Plants

		Flower Color	Time of Bloom	Growth Habit	Hardiness	Growing Conditions
PENSTEMON SOUTHWESTERN PENSTEMON ◄ *Penstemon barbatus* SHOWY PENSTEMON *P. spectabilis*	Tall, western natives with showy, tubular, 2-lipped flowers atop erect stems. P. barbatus has bright red-orange, 1-in. flowers and deep green, grassy leaves; P. spectabilis, 1- to 1½-in. pink to violet flowers and coarsely toothed leaves.	○ ● ● ● ●	P. barb. Summer to mid-autumn P. spec. Mid-spring to early summer	P. barb. Height: 2–6' Spread: 1–2' P. spec. Height: 2–4' Spread: 1–1½'	P. barb. 5 to 9 P. spec. 9 to 10 (Grow as an annual in colder regions)	Full sun to very light shade. Well-drained, dry soil. Penstemon will not tolerate wet soil. Plants are ideal for rock gardens.
PHACELIA CALIFORNIA BLUEBELL *Phacelia campanularia*	A native California annual with deep blue, 1- to 1½-in., bell-shaped flowers in open, branched clusters atop hairy, erect stems. Toothed, round, 1-in. leaves are also covered with soft hairs.	●	Midwinter to mid-spring	Height: 6–24" Spread: 6–24"	Tender annual	Full sun. Sandy, well-drained, nutrient-poor soil. Although a desert species, Phacelia can be grown easily in the garden as long as the soil is not too wet. The flowering season is prolonged when the weather is cool.
PHLOX BLUE PHLOX ◄ *Phlox divaricata* CREEPING PHLOX *P. stolonifera*	Perennials with fragrant lavender-blue flowers and oval leaves. P. divaricata has loose clusters of 1½-in. flowers with notched petals; the mat-forming P. stolonifera has 1-in. flowers with smooth petals and fewer flowers per cluster.	○ ○	Early spring to early summer	P. div. Height: 8–18" Spread: 8–12" P. stol. Height: 4–6" Spread: 1–2'	4 to 8	Filtered sun to full shade. Well-drained, evenly moist, humus-rich, slightly acid soil. These phlox are excellent plants for shady rock gardens or for naturalizing in woodland settings.
PHLOX ANNUAL PHLOX *Phlox drummondii*	An annual phlox native to eastern Texas, with dense, branched clusters of brilliant pink, red, purple, or white 5-petaled, tubular flowers atop erect stems. The stems and 1- to 2-in. leaves are covered with sticky hairs.	○ ○ ● ●	Spring to late summer	Height: 6–18" Spread: 6–12"	Tender annual	Full sun. Well-drained soil. In zone 8 and warmer, sow seeds outdoors in autumn; elsewhere start seeds indoors 8 weeks before last frost. Prolong the flowering season by deadheading and providing additional moisture.
PHYSOSTEGIA OBEDIENT PLANT, FALSE DRAGONHEAD *Physostegia virginiana*	A native perennial useful in borders or meadows. Lance-shaped deep green leaves clasp square stems that are topped by conical spires of pink, white, or lavender, tubular, 2-lipped flowers. When bent, flowers retain their new positions.	○ ○ ○	Midsummer to early autumn	Height: 2–4' Spread: 1–2'	3 to 8	Full sun to partial shade, with shade in zone 7 and warmer. Average soil conditions. Physostegia is easy to grow and tolerates nutrient-poor and damp soil.

		Flower Color	Time of Bloom	Growth Habit	Hardiness	Growing Conditions

PHYTOLACCA
POKEWEED
Phytolacca americana

A tall native perennial with crimson stems; oval, 6- to 8-in., light green leaves; and 6-in. racemes of ¼-in. flowers. Each flower has 5 white petal-like sepals and a green center and produces blue-black berries in fall. Roots and berries are poisonous.

Flower Color: ○ | Time of Bloom: Summer | Growth Habit: Height: 3–12' Spread: 1–3' | Hardiness: 4 to 10 | Growing Conditions: Full sun to light shade. A wide variety of soils. Pokeweed may become weedy where soil is fertile and moist and where the climate is sunny.

PODOPHYLLUM
MAYAPPLE
Podophyllum peltatum

A perennial with pairs of 6- to 12-in., rounded, lobed leaves between which a single, waxy, fragrant, white, 2-in., nodding flower emerges in spring. The 1- to 2-in. green fruit that follows is edible; the rest of the plant is poisonous.

Flower Color: ○ | Time of Bloom: Mid-spring | Growth Habit: Height: 1–1½' Spread: 1–2' | Hardiness: 3 to 8 | Growing Conditions: Full sun to light shade. Evenly moist, humus-rich, moderately acid to neutral soil that never completely dries out. Mayapple adapts to even shady gardens and makes an excellent, though tall, ground cover.

POLEMONIUM
JACOB'S-LADDER
◁ *Polemonium caeruleum*
GREEK VALERIAN
P. reptans

Woodland perennials native to eastern U.S. Attractive ladderlike leaves grow on lower halves of long stems with loose clusters of bell-shaped blue (or sometimes white), 5-petaled, ½-in. flowers. P. reptans is smaller and more sprawling.

Flower Color: ○ ● | Time of Bloom: Late spring to late summer | Growth Habit: Height: 1½–2½' Spread: 8–12" | Hardiness: 2 to 7 | Growing Conditions: Full sun to partial shade. Well-drained soil that is evenly moist and rich in humus. Mulch during winter in cooler climates.

POLYGONATUM
SMALL SOLOMON'S-SEAL
◁ *Polygonatum biflorum*
GREAT SOLOMON'S-SEAL
P. commutatum

Eastern woodland native perennials grown more for their foliage and pairs of blue-black berries than for the ½- to 1-in.; yellow-green, tubular flowers dangling below arching stems. P. commutatum is a giant version of P. biflorum.

Flower Color: ● | Time of Bloom: Spring | Growth Habit: P. bifl. Height: 1–2½' Spread: 1–1½' P. comm. Height: 3–6' Spread: 2–3' | Hardiness: 3 to 8 | Growing Conditions: Partial sun to full shade in humus-rich, well-drained, evenly moist soil that never completely dries out. Polygonatum may be troubled by slugs and snails.

POTENTILLA
ROUGH-FRUITED CINQUEFOIL
Potentilla recta

A perennial member of the rose family with 5-petaled, yellow, ½- to 1-in. flowers. As with other cinquefoils, P. recta has compound leaves with 5 to 7 toothed, spatula-shaped segments. Plants have an erect form.

Time of Bloom: Summer | Growth Habit: Height: 1–2' Spread: 4–8" | Hardiness: 4 to 8 | Growing Conditions: Full sun. Well-drained, evenly moist, slightly alkaline soil. P. recta adapts to a wide range of conditions and may become weedy.

◁ *Indicates species shown*

Wildflowers & Native Plants

			Flower Color	Time of Bloom	Growth Habit	Hardiness	Growing Conditions
RATIBIDA MEXICAN HAT *Ratibida columnifera* *(R. columnaris)* PRAIRIE CONEFLOWER ◁ *R. pinnata*		Perennials native to prairies and plains whose 1- to 3-in. flowers have conical centers and drooping ray petals. R. columnifera has a 1- to 2-in.-high cone and either yellow or red ray petals; R. pinnata has a shorter cone and yellow ray petals.	●	Summer to early autumn	R. colum. Height: 1–3' Spread: 6–18" R. pinn. Height: 3–5' Spread: 1–3'	5 to 9	Full sun. Well-drained soil. Both species adapt well to garden soil conditions. Once established they are drought tolerant, especially R. columnifera.
RHEXIA MEADOW BEAUTY *Rhexia virginica*		One of the most beautiful native perennials of wet prairies and meadows. It bears clusters of exquisite 1- to 1½-in. flowers with 4 rose-crimson petals surrounding a yellow pistil and prominent golden stamens. Fruits resemble copper urns.	●	Midsummer to early autumn	Height: 4–30" Spread: 4–12"	5 to 9	Full sun to light shade. Wet to moist, acid soil. Rhexia does not tolerate dry soil but will grow under boggy conditions.
ROMNEYA CALIFORNIA TREE POPPY, MATILIJA POPPY *Romneya coulteri*		A magnificent poppy with smooth blue-gray leaves that are irregularly divided. Handsome 4- to 6-in. flowers have 6 white petals with the texture of crepe paper. At the flower centers are masses of golden yellow stamens.	○	Late spring to summer	Height: 3–8' Spread: 1–3"	8 to 11	Full sun. Well-drained soil. Romneya adapts well to garden soil conditions. Once established it is drought tolerant. With time, plants will form large shrublike clumps from underground rhizomes.
RUDBECKIA BLACK-EYED SUSAN *Rudbeckia hirta*		A popular midwestern native perennial usually grown as an annual. Daisylike, 2- to 3-in. flowers have deep yellow outer petals and dark brown, silky, domed centers. The fuzzy, 3- to 4-in. leaves are scattered along the hairy, upright stems.		Summer to early autumn	Height: 1–3' Spread: 6–18"	3 to 9	Full sun to very light shade. Well-drained soil. Black-eyed Susan reseeds once established and may become weedy in the garden. Young plants propagated from seed flower later in the season. Rudbeckia is ideal for meadows.
RUELLIA WILD PETUNIA ◁ *Ruellia caroliniensis* *R. humulis*		Perennials native to the Midwest and Southeast with lancelike leaves. Showy, 1- to 2-in., funnel-shaped, 5-lobed, lilac-blue flowers emerge from where upper leaves join the hairy stems. R. humulis is shorter and has smaller leaves.	●	Summer	Height: 1–2' Spread: 1–1½'	5 to 9	Full sun to very light shade. Well-drained, sandy soil. Ruellia is a plant native to dry prairies and open woodlands.

		Flower Color	Time of Bloom	Growth Habit	Hardiness	Growing Conditions
SALVIA BLUE SAGE *Salvia azurea* SCARLET SAGE ◄ *S. coccinea*	Native perennials with 2-lipped, tubular flowers on square, slender, erect stems. S. azurea has ½-in. light blue, dark blue, or white flowers whorled around the stem tops; S. coccinea has 1-in. bright scarlet flowers in loose spikes.	● ○ ●	Late spring to frost	S. azur. Height: 1–6' Spread: 1–2' S. cocc. Height: 1–2' Spread: 6–12"	S. azur. 4 to 9 S. cocc. 9 to 11 (Grow as an annual elsewhere)	Full sun. Well-drained, evenly moist soil. Once established, both species are drought tolerant. S. coccinea is easily grown as an annual by sowing seeds outdoors in spring.
SANGUINARIA BLOODROOT *Sanguinaria canadensis*	An eastern woodland perennial with flower stalks rising from 4- to 8-in., round, scalloped leaves. Single, 8-petaled, 2- to 3-in. white flowers last about a week and then produce 2- to 4-in. green pods. Roots and stems contain red sap.	○	Late winter to early spring	Height: 6–15" Spread: 1–2'	6 to 9	Full sun to deep shade; sites under deciduous trees and shrubs are ideal. Humus-rich, moist, well-drained soil. Bloodroot spreads slowly, forming an attractive ground cover for most of the summer. Provide winter mulch in zones 3–4.
SAPONARIA BOUNCING BET, SOAPWORT *Saponaria officinalis*	Stout, branching perennial with clusters of white or pink, 1-in., tubular flowers with 5 narrow, scalloped lobes. Pairs of smooth, 3- to 4-in. leaves clasp the stem. The sap was once used as a soaplike foam.	○ ●	Summer to early autumn	Height: 1–3' Spread: 6–12"	3 to 10	Full sun to light shade. Not at all particular about soil conditions. This European native colonizes disturbed areas and may become weedy.
SARRACENIA TRUMPET PITCHER PLANT ◄ *Sarracenia flava* COMMON PITCHER PLANT *S. purpurea*	Perennials with fluid-filled leaves that digest insects. S. flava has big, erect, trumpet-shaped, red-tinged, yellow leaves; S. purpurea has floppier leaves variegated with or entirely purple. Umbrella-like flowers have the same colors as leaves.	● ●	Mid- to late spring	S. flav. Height: 1–3' Spread: 6–18" S. purp. Height: 8–24" Spread: 1–2'	S. flav. 7 to 9 S. purp. 4 to 9	Full sun to light shade. Moist to constantly wet, acid, boggy soil. Native to eastern bogs, pitcher plants do not tolerate dry or alkaline soil.
SEDUM PACIFIC SEDUM ◄ *Sedum spathulifolium* WILD STONECROP *S. ternatum*	Low-growing perennial succulents with oval, ½- to 1-in. leaves and flowers with 5 pointed petals. S. spathulifolium has branching clusters of ¾-in. yellow flowers above rosettes of leaves. S. ternatum has sprays of white flowers on trailing stems.	○	S. spath. Mid- to late spring S. tern. Late spring to summer	S. spath. Height: 4–8" Spread: 6–12" S. tern. Height: 4–12" Spread: 4–8"	S. spath. 5 to 7 S. tern. 8 to 10	S. spathulifolium: Pacific Coast native; full sun; well-drained, sandy, rocky, or gravelly soil. S. ternatum: native to open, deciduous woodlands in the East; partial shade; humus-rich, evenly moist, slightly acid soil.

◄ Indicates species shown

Wildflowers & Native Plants

		Flower Color	Time of Bloom	Growth Habit	Hardiness	Growing Conditions
SENECIO GOLDEN RAGWORT *Senecio aureus*	A native eastern woodland perennial bearing flat-topped clusters of 8 to 12, golden, ³/₄-in., daisylike flowers in late spring. The leaves are heart-shaped at the bottom of smooth stems, becoming smaller and ferny toward the tops.		Mid- to late spring	Height: 1–3' Spread: 3–8"	4 to 9	Full sun to shade. Moist to wet, humus-rich soil. Senecio is an excellent plant for naturalizing in damp woodlands.
SHORTIA OCONEE-BELLS *Shortia galacifolia*	An Appalachian perennial that is rare in the wild but often found in gardens. Glossy, round, 3-in., ever-green leaves redden in winter. Erect 5- to 8-in. stems bear 1-in., nodding, white or pink, 5-lobed flowers.	○ ●	Early to mid-spring	Height: 4–8" Spread: 3–6"	6 to 9	Light shade to full shade. Humus-rich, evenly moist, acid, well-drained soil; sandy loam with added humus is ideal. Shortia needs constant moisture but will not tolerate soggy conditions. Propagate by division in spring.
SILENE BLADDER CAMPION *Silene cucubalus* FIRE PINK ◄ *S. virginica*	Perennials in the pink family that have flowers with 5 deeply cleft petals and pairs of leaves that clasp sticky-haired stems. S. cucubalus has white flowers with round, inflated, green bases. S. virginica has bright scarlet flowers with narrow petals.	○ ●	S. cucub. Late spring to late summer S. virg. Late spring to mid-summer	S. cucub. Height: 1–2' Spread: 6–12" S. virg. Height: 1–2' Spread: 1–2'	S. cucub. 4 to 9 S. virg. 7 to 9	Full sun to partial shade. Average garden or meadow soil. S. cucubalis is a European native that naturalizes in roadside areas. S. virginica, native to southeastern open woodlands, prefers light shade or filtered sun.
SISYRINCHIUM EASTERN BLUE-EYED GRASS ◄ *Sisyrinchium angustifolium* WESTERN BLUE-EYED GRASS *S. bellum*	Clump-forming native perennials of the iris family with grasslike leaves and narrow stems that bear clusters of ¹/₂-in. blue flowers with yellow centers. After the flowers wither, the plant blends into the grassy landscape.	●	Mid-spring	Height: 5–15" Spread: 6–12"	S. ang. 3 to 8 S. bell. 8 to 11	Full sun to partial shade. Average garden or meadow soil. The hardier S. angusti-folium, an eastern native, is good for meadows. S. bellum does best in mild climates; it needs moisture in the growing season and drier soil after flowering.
SMILACINA FALSE SOLOMON'S-SEAL, SOLOMON'S-PLUMES *Smilacina racemosa*	A woodland native perennial with a spikelike cluster of tiny, white, foamy flowers at the tip of each arching stem. The 3- to 6-in. clasping leaves are often purple where they meet the stem. Red berries appear in summer.	○	Mid-spring to early summer	Height: 1–2¹/₂' Spread: 9–12"	3 to 9	Dappled sun to full shade, with some afternoon shade in warm climates. Well-drained, evenly moist, humus-rich soil. Smilacina will grow in full sun but will be smaller. Mulch plants during winter in cooler climates.

		Flower Color	Time of Bloom	Growth Habit	Hardiness	Growing Conditions
SOLIDAGO GOLDENROD ◀ *Solidago canadensis* SWEET GOLDENROD *S. odora*	Perennials with ¼- to ⅓-in. golden yellow flowers in dense, 4- to 5-in. spikes atop woody stems. S. canadensis has toothed leaves, 6 in. at the stem's bottom and smaller at the top; S. odora has smooth, narrow, anise-scented leaves.		Late summer to early autumn	S. canad. Height: 1½–5' Spread: 1–1½' S. odora Height: 1½–3' Spread: 1–1½'	3 to 9	Full sun. Well-drained soil of average to poor fertility. These species are clump forming and spread only slowly. The heavy pollen of goldenrods does not cause hay fever, contrary to popular belief.
SPIGELIA PINKROOT *Spigelia marilandica*	A southeastern native wood-land perennial bearing 1-in., upright, tubular, scarlet flowers, each divided into 5 sharp, narrow lobes that reveal the yellow insides of the petals. Pairs of 4-in. leaves clasp the stem.	●	Late spring to summer	Height: 1–2' Spread: 6–18"	6 to 9	Filtered sun to shade. Humus-rich, evenly moist, fertile soil; sites under decid-uous trees are ideal. Spigelia is excellent for naturalizing in southern woodlands.
STOKESIA STOKES'S ASTER *Stokesia laevis*	A southeastern native perennial with spectacular ragged-petaled, clear blue, 2- to 3-in. flower heads that have lighter centers and are borne on branched stems with shiny deep green leaves.	●	Summer	Height: 1–2' Spread: 6–12"	5 to 9	Full sun to partial shade. Well-drained, evenly moist soil. Once established, Stokesia is relatively drought tolerant. Plants may be trou-bled by slugs and snails. Mulch during winter in zone 6 and colder.
THALICTRUM EARLY MEADOW RUE *Thalictrum dioicum* TALL MEADOW RUE ◀ *T. polygamum*	Native perennials with deli-cate compound leaves with rounded lobes and clusters of greenish white, petalless flowers with threadlike sta-mens. T. dioicum has droop-ing flowers on long stems; T. polygamum has plumes of starry flowers.	●	T. dio. Mid- to late spring T. poly. Late spring to late summer	T. dio. Height: 1–2' Spread: 1–2' T. poly. Height: 2–8' Spread: 1–2'	4 to 8	Full sun to shade. Moist, humus-rich, fertile soil; sites under deciduous trees are ideal. T. dioicum grows best in neutral to alkaline soil and benefits from additions of ground limestone. T. poly-gamum tolerates wet soil.
THERMOPSIS CAROLINA LUPINE, FALSE LUPINE *Thermopsis caroliniana* (T. villosa)	A native of the pea family with erect racemes of light yellow flowers at the tops of stiff stems. Compound leaves have 3 gray-green leaflets.		Summer	Height: 3–5' Spread: 1–1½'	3 to 8	Full sun to partial shade. Well-drained, evenly moist soil. The deep roots of Thermopsis make it relatively drought tolerant once estab-lished. Propagate by division, as the seeds are slow to germinate.

◀ *Indicates species shown*

Wildflowers & Native Plants

		Flower Color	Time of Bloom	Growth Habit	Hardiness	Growing Conditions
TIARELLA FOAMFLOWER *Tiarella cordifolia*	Evergreen perennial ground cover forming mounds of fuzzy, heart-shaped, light green leaves that turn bronze in autumn. The frothy spikes of 5-petaled, white flowers are held above the foliage.	○	Late spring	Height: 8–12" Spread: 9–15"	3 to 8	Partial sun to full shade. Moist, humus-rich soil; sites under deciduous trees are ideal. Foamflower will not tolerate dry soil but will adapt to normal garden conditions if shade is provided. Slugs can be a problem.
TRADES-CANTIA SPIDERWORT *Tradescantia virginiana*	An eastern native bearing circular clusters of many 3-petaled blue flowers with golden anthers. Blue-green grasslike leaves up to 15 in. long clasp the stems. The flowers open in the morning and last only a day.	○ ◉ ◉	Late spring to mid-summer	Height: 1–2' Spread: 1–1½'	3 to 9	Full sun to partial shade. Well-drained, but moist, humus-rich soil. Mulch plants during winter in cooler climates. Divide clumps every several years to keep them flowering vigorously.
TRILLIUM NODDING TRILLIUM ◀ *Trillium cernuum* PURPLE TRILLIUM *T. erectum*	Native perennials with whorls of 3 broad, diamond-shaped leaves and 3-petaled flowers. T. cernuum has ¾-in. white flowers on curved stalks below the leaves; T. erectum has 1- to 2-in. maroon flowers above the leaves.	○ ●	Spring	Height: 1–2' Spread: 6–18"	3 to 8	Partial sun to full shade. Humus-rich, evenly moist soil that never dries out completely; sites under deciduous trees are ideal. T. cernuum prefers acid soil. T. erectum grows best in soil that is near neutral.
TRILLIUM WHITE WAKE-ROBIN ◀ *Trillium grandiflorum* PAINTED TRILLIUM *T. undulatum*	Showy native perennials with wavy-petaled flowers on erect stalks above whorls of 3 leaves. T. grandiflorum has 2- to 3-in. flowers that turn deep pink with age. T. undulatum has 1-in. white flowers with pink stripes.	○ ◉	Spring	T. grand. Height: 1–2' Spread: 6–18" T. und. Height: 6–12" Spread: 6–12"	3 to 8	Partial sun to full shade. Humus-rich, evenly moist soil that never dries out completely; sites under deciduous trees are ideal. T. grandiflorum prefers slightly acid soil. T. undulatum grows best in soil that is close to neutral.
UVULARIA LARGE-FLOWERED BELLWORT *Uvularia grandiflora* PERFOLIATE BELLWORT ◀ *U. perfoliata*	Native woodland perennials whose 6-part, drooping yellow flowers never seem to open fully. U. grandiflora is larger, with 2-in. bright yellow flowers. U. perfoliata has 1-in. pale yellow flowers and leaf bases that encircle the stems.		Spring	U. grand. Height: 1½–2½' Spread: 1–2' U. perf. Height: 1–2' Spread: 1–2'	4 to 8	Partial sun to full shade. Humus-rich, evenly moist soil that never dries out completely; sites under deciduous trees are ideal. Uvularia spreads with age and benefits slowly from division every several years.

		Flower Color	Time of Bloom	Growth Habit	Hardiness	Growing Conditions
VERBASCUM COMMON MULLEIN *Verbascum thapsus*	A bold biennial with striking, 4- to 12-in., fuzzy, gray-green leaves that form a low rosette the first year. The second year a long wandlike stem emerges bearing yellow, 1-in., often sticky flowers.		Summer	Height: 2–6' Spread: 1–2'	3 to 8	Full sun to light shade. Well-drained soil of average fertility. Mullein, a Eurasian species, has naturalized in nearly every locale where winters are cool enough to stimulate flowering the second year. It is prone to root rot if soil is too wet.
VERBENA ROSE VERBENA, ROSE VERVAIN *Verbena canadensis*	A low, creeping southeastern native. Rose, lilac, or white, ½-in., 5-lobed flowers in dense, flat-topped clusters at the ends of hairy, trailing stems. The leaves are 2- to 4-in. ovals with flattened bases.	○ ● ●	Spring to summer	Height: 6–18" Spread: 1–2'	6 to 9	Full sun to light shade. Well-drained, evenly moist garden soil. Rose verbena adapts to dry soil as well; plants are drought tolerant once established.
VERNONIA IRONWEED *Vernonia noveboracensis*	A tall, clumping perennial native to moist meadows, thickets, and streamsides in the East. Clusters of many ½-in., shaggy, purple flowers bloom atop erect stems bearing narrow, lance-shaped, 4- to 8-in. leaves.	●	Late summer to early autumn	Height: 4–6' Spread: 2–4'	5 to 9	Full sun to light shade. Moist, humus-rich soil that never dries out completely. Vernonia can be grown as a border plant, but it needs plenty of space, since it spreads with age.
VIOLA SWEET WHITE VIOLET *Viola blanda* COMMON BLUE VIOLET ◀ *V. sororia*	Eastern woodland natives with mounds of heart-shaped leaves and fragrant, 5-petaled flowers. V. blanda has ½-in. white flowers, each with 4 bent-back upper petals and a purple-striped lower petal. V. sororia has deep purple flowers.	○ ● ●	Spring	V. bland. Height: 2–6" Spread: 3–6" V. pap. Height: 4–8" Spread: 6–12"	3 to 8	Full sun to shade. Evenly moist, humus-rich soil that never completely dries out; sites under deciduous trees and shrubs are ideal. These highly adaptable species can become a bit weedy in the garden but are ideal for naturalizing in woodland gardens.
VIOLA BIRD'S-FOOT VIOLET ◀ *Viola pedata* SMOOTH YELLOW VIOLET *V. pubescens* var. *eriocarpa* (*V. pensylvanica*)	Native violets found in open areas and woods. V. pedata has 1-in.-wide, lilac or purple, flat, pansylike flowers and 1- to 2-in.-wide, deeply cut leaves. V. pubescens var. eriocarpa has ½-in. yellow flowers with dark purple veins.	● ●	Mid- to late spring	V. ped. Height: 2–6" Spread: 3–8" V. pub. Height: 4–16" Spread: 6–12"	3 to 8	Full sun to shade. Evenly moist, humus-rich soil; sites under deciduous trees and shrubs are ideal.

◀ Indicates species shown

Wildflowers & Native Plants

		Flower Color	Time of Bloom	Growth Habit	Hardiness	Growing Conditions
XEROPHYLLUM BEAR GRASS *Xerophyllum tenax*	A perennial native to Pacific Northwest woodlands. It has clumps of narrow (¹⁄₁₀-in.-wide), wiry, 1- to 2-ft.-long grasslike leaves. Shoots with 3- to 6-in. domed clusters of fragrant, ¼-in., 6-part white flowers emerge from foliage.	○	Late spring to mid-summer	Height: 2–5' Spread: 2–3'	4 to 10	Full sun to light shade. Moist, well-drained, acid, humus-rich soil.
YUCCA ADAM'S-NEEDLE *Yucca filamentosa*	A southeastern native perennial that forms clumps of tough, 2-ft.-long, spine-tipped, gray-green leaves. A tall, branched stalk bears many waxy, white, 2-in., fragrant flowers. Plant center dies after flowering, but offsets will flourish.	○	Summer	Height: 5–12' Spread: 3–6'	5 to 11	Full sun to very light shade. Well-drained, sandy or gravelly soil. Yucca is drought tolerant but will not tolerate soggy soils. Mulch during winter in zone 7 and colder.
ZAUSCHNERIA CALIFORNIA FUCHSIA *Zauschneria californica*	A native perennial of southern California with sprawling masses of gray-green, ½- to 1-in., woolly leaves. The foliage is evergreen in zones 10–11, contrasting with vermilion, tubular, 2-lipped, 1- to 1½-in. flowers.	● ●	Summer to late autumn	Height: 6–18" Spread: 1–3'	9 to 11	Full sun. Well-drained, sandy or gravelly, slightly alkaline soil. Plants are drought tolerant and rot if soil is too moist. Zauschneria spreads rapidly and makes an ideal ground cover in hot, sunny climates.
ZEPHYRAN-THES ATAMASCO LILY *Zephyranthes atamasco*	A perennial bulb native to wet woods and meadows of the Southeast. The 2- to 3-in.-long, 6-lobed, waxy, white, erect, lilylike flowers rise on leafless stalks among 1-ft., grasslike, grooved leaves. Atamasco lily is in the amaryllis family.	○	Spring	Height: 8–12" Spread: 3–6"	7 to 9	Full sun to shade. Evenly moist to wet, humus-rich soil. Zephyranthes will not tolerate cold winters or soil that dries out completely.
ZINNIA PLAINS ZINNIA, DESERT ZINNIA *Zinnia grandiflora*	A colorful shrubby perennial native to the Great Plains. The 1- to 1½-in. flowers have rounded yellow ray petals and green or red centers. The needlelike, 1-in. leaves become twisted with age.		Spring to mid-autumn	Height: 4–10" Spread: 6–18"	6 to 10	Full sun. Dry, well-drained, sandy soil. Plains zinnias are tolerant of both drought and alkaline soil and have a long flowering season.

Plant Hardiness Zone Map

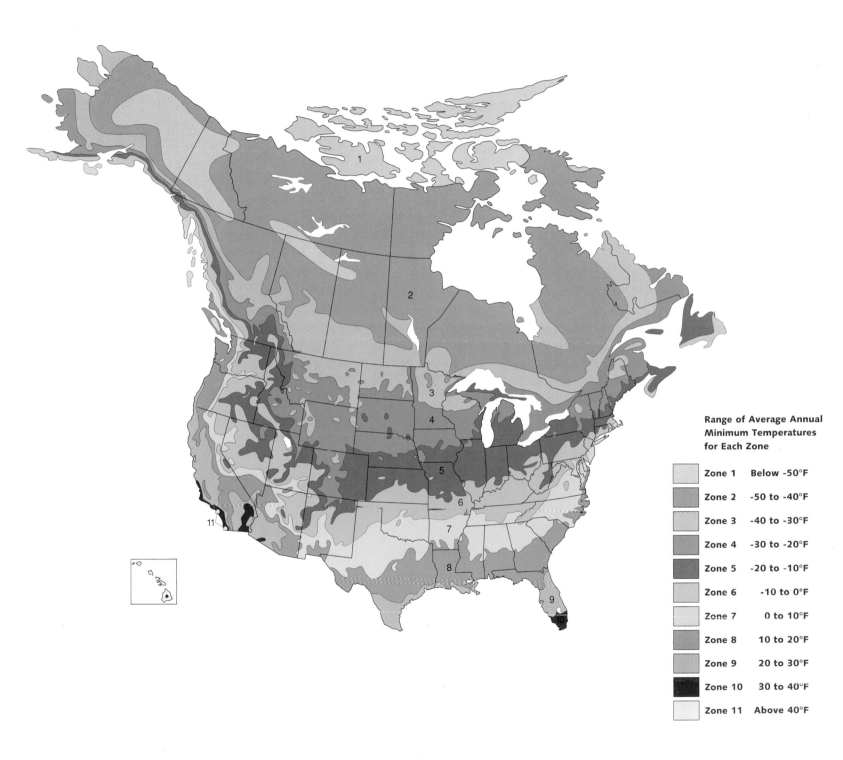

Range of Average Annual Minimum Temperatures for Each Zone

	Zone 1	Below -50°F
	Zone 2	-50 to -40°F
	Zone 3	-40 to -30°F
	Zone 4	-30 to -20°F
	Zone 5	-20 to -10°F
	Zone 6	-10 to 0°F
	Zone 7	0 to 10°F
	Zone 8	10 to 20°F
	Zone 9	20 to 30°F
	Zone 10	30 to 40°F
	Zone 11	Above 40°F

Resources for Gardening with Wildflowers & Native Plants

There are many dependable mail-order suppliers that can be helpful for gardeners interested in wildflowers and native plants. A selection is included here. Most have catalogues available upon request (some charge a fee). An excellent source of further resources is Gardening by Mail by Barbara J. Barton. Updates on each edition are provided three times a year, available through subscription (forms provided in back of book); a new edition comes out every few years. To obtain this book, check your local bookstore or contact the publisher: Houghton Mifflin Co., 222 Berkeley Street, Boston, MA 02116. Telephone: (617) 351-5000.

Seeds & Plants

Abundant Life Seed
Foundation
P.O. Box 772
Port Townsend,
WA 98368
206-385-7192
Over 600 varieties of open-pollinated, chemical-free seeds.

Clyde Robin Seed Co.
P.O. Box 2366
Castro Valley, CA 94546
800-647-6475
Color catalogue of seeds and wildflower mixtures.

DeGiorgi Seeds & Goods
6011 'N' Street
Omaha, NE 68117-1634
800-858-2580
Broad selection of seeds, including many natives.

Forest Farm
990 Tetherow Road
Williams, OR 97544
503-846-6963
Native perennials, trees, and shrubs.

Holbrook Farm & Nursery
115 Lance Road
P.O. Box 368
Fletcher, NC 28732
704-891-7790
Catalogue of perennials with a section on native plants.

J. L. Hudson, Seedsman
P.O. Box 1058
Redwood City, CA 94064
Large collection of rare seeds. No phone orders.

Mellinger's Inc.
2310 W. South Range Road
North Lima, OH 44452
800-321-7444
Seeds, plants, supplies, and tools.

Moon Mountain
P.O. Box 34
Morro Bay, CA 93443
805-772-2473
Catalogue featuring many seeds and seed mixtures.

Native Gardens
5737 Fisher Lane
Greenback, TN 37742
615-856-0220
Catalogue featuring nursery-propagated native perennials.

Niche Gardens
111 Dawson Road
Chapel Hill, NC 27516
919-967-0078
Catalogue of nursery-propagated wildflowers with advice on most suitable sites.

Nichols Garden Nursery
1190 N. Pacific Highway
Albany, OR 97321-4598
503-928-9280
Seeds for herbs and everlastings as well as books and supplies.

Peaceful Valley Farm
Supply
P.O. Box 2209
Grass Valley, CA 95945
916-272-4769
Wildflowers, bulbs, and native perennials.

Richters
357 Highway 47
Goodwood, Ontario
Canada LOC 1AO
416-640-6677
Seeds of herbs, everlasting flowers, and wildflowers.

Siskiyou Rare Plant
Nursery
2825 Cummings Road
Medford, OR 97501
503-772-6846
Wide variety of native plants.

Thompson & Morgan
P.O. Box 1308
Jackson, NJ 08527-0308
800-274-7333
Natives and a wide range of other garden supplies.

Vermont Wildflower Farm
Route 7, Box 5
Charlotte, VT 05445
802-425-3500
Wildflower seeds and mixes for sun or shade.

Wildlife Nurseries, Inc.
P.O. Box 2724
Oshkosh, WI 54903
414-231-3780
Many native plants, including those that attract backyard wildlife.

Wildseed Farms, Inc.
1101 Campo Rosa Road
Eagle Lake, TX 77454
800-848-0078
Color catalogue featuring seeds and wildflower mixes.

Regional Specialties

Boothe Hill Wildflowers
23B Boothe Hill Road
Chapel Hill, NC 27514
919-967-4091
Native seeds and plants that perform well in the Southeast.

High Altitude Gardens
P.O. Box 1048
Hailey, ID 83333
208-788-4363
Seeds, including natives, selected for their ability to grow at high altitudes.

Native Seeds/SEARCH
2509 N. Campbell,
No. 325
Tucson, AZ 85719
602-327-9123
Native seeds of the
Southwest and Mexico,
collected and propagated
with long-term preserva-
tion in mind and distrib-
uted free to Native
Americans.

Prairie Nursery
Wildflowers
P.O. Box 306
Westfield, WI 53964
608-296-3679
Specializing in prairie
plants, seeds, and native
grasses.

Redwood City Seed Co.
P.O. Box 361
Redwood City, CA 94064
415-325-7333
Native western U.S. vari-
eties, including grasses.

Shooting Star Nursery
444 Bates Road
Frankfort, KY 40601
502-223-1679
Over 200 species native to
the eastern states.

Sunlight Gardens
174 Golden Lane
Andersonville, TN 37705
800-272-7396
Catalogue of native plants
of eastern North America,
including trees and shrubs.

Wild Seed, Inc.
P.O. Box 27751
Tempe, AZ 85285
602-345-0669
Wide variety of wildflower
seeds for the Southwest.

Supplies & Accessories

Erth-Rite
RD 1, Box 243
Gap, PA 17527
800-332-4171
Soil amendments.

Garden Way, Inc.
102nd Street & 9th
Avenue
Troy, NY 12180
800-833-6990
Mowers, rotary tillers,
garden carts, and various
other lawn and garden
equipment.

Gardener's Eden
P.O. Box 7303
San Francisco, CA 94120
800-822-9600
Many items appropriate
for gardeners, including
outdoor containers, tools,
and accessories.

Gardener's Supply Co.
128 Intervale Rd.
Burlington, VT 05401
800-876-5520
Products, gifts, greenhouse
kits, and composting
equipment.

Gardens Alive!
5100 Schenley Place
Lawrenceburg, IN 47025
812-537-8650
Beneficial insects and a
complete line of supplies
for organic gardening.

Home Gardener
Manufacturing Company
30 Wright Avenue
Lititz, PA 17543
800-880-2345
Composting and home
gardening equipment.

Plow & Hearth
P.O. Box 830
Orange, VA 22960
800-866-6072
Gardening tools and prod-
ucts, garden ornaments,
and furniture.

Ringer Corporation
9959 Valley View Road
Eden Prairie, MN 55344
612-941-4180
Organic soil amendments,
beneficial insects, and garden tools.

Smith & Hawken
Two Arbor Lane
Box 6900
Florence, KY 41022-6900
800-776-3336
Well-crafted tools as well
as clothing, containers,
supplies, and furniture.

Information Sources

Canadian Wildflower
Society
1220 Fieldstone Circle
Pickering, Ontario
L1X 1B4
Conducts a native plant
seed exchange.

Eastern Native Plant
Alliance
Adkins Aboretum
P.O. Box 147
Hillsboro, MD 21641
410-634-2847
Serves as a forum to share
ideas and information
about native plants.

Ecological Stewardship
Services
444 Bates Road
Frankfort, KY 40601
505-223-1679
Full range of consulting
services for ecological gardening and landscaping.

National Wildflower
Research Center
4801 La Crosse Boulevard
Austin, TX 78739
512-292-4100
Provides information and
conducts research on
native plants.

New England Wild Flower
Society
180 Hemenway Road
Framingham, MA 01701
508-877-7630
Catalogue featuring nurs-
ery sources of native
plants and wildflowers for
the entire country.

Theodore Payne
Foundation
10459 Tuxford Street
Sun Valley, CA 91352
818-768-1802
Dedicated to the preserva-
tion and use of
California's native plants.

Index

Photo Credits

All photography credited as follows is copyright © 1995 by the individual photographers. **Agri-Starts III:** p. 49; **Henry W. Art:** pp. 76 (right), 77 (all); **W. D. Bransford (courtesy of National Wildflower Research Center):** p. 20; **Karen Bussolini:** pp. 12, 17, 21 (top), 27, 76 (left and center); **David Cavagnaro:** pp. 26, 29; **Walter Chandoha:** pp. 7, 19, 34, 81; **Christine Douglas:** p. 4; **Ken Druse/The Natural Garden:** pp. 35, 78; **Derek Fell:** pp. 48, 61; **Pamela Harper:** p. 87; **Dency Kane:** p. 88; **Peter Loewer:** p. 25; **Maggie Oster:** pp. 44, 59, 66; **Jerry Pavia:** p. 32; **Joanne Pavia:** p. 65; **Susan Roth:** pp. 9, 11 (all), 16 (right), 50, 84, 90; **Michael S. Thompson:** pp. 16 (left), 21 (bottom), 28.

Step-by-step photography by **Derek Fell.**

Front cover photograph copyright © 1995 by **Ken Druse/The Natural Garden.**

All plant encyclopedia photography is copyright © 1995 by **Derek Fell,** except the following, which are copyright © 1995 by the individual photographers. **Henry W. Art:** *Baileya multiradiata, Collinsia heterophylla, Gilia rubra, Hypericum perforatum, Lasthenia chrysostoma, Linanthus grandiflorus, Mentzelia lindleyi, Mimulus aurantiacus;* **Suzanne F. Bales:** *Sanguinaria canadensis, Tradescantia virginiana;* **Jean Baxter (courtesy of New England Wild Flower Society, Inc.):** *Thalictrum polygamum;* **Frank Bramley (courtesy of New England Wild Flower Society, Inc.):** *Acorus americanus;* **Michael Dirr:** *Actaea rubra, Baptisia australis,* *Chimaphila maculata, Clintonia umbellulata, Dionaea muscipula, Gillenia trifoliata, Hypoxis hirsuta, Jeffersonia diphylla, Senecio aureus, Smilacina racemosa, Spigelia marilandica, Trillium cernuum, Verbena canadensis;* **Susan M. Glascock:** *Abronia villosa, Drosera rotundifolia, Lewisia rediviva, Mitchella repens, Podophyllum peltatum;* **Pamela Harper:** *Achillea millefolium, Brodiaea hyacinthina, Calla palustris, Chamaelirium luteum, Erigeron glaucus, Galax urceolata, Gaultheria procumbens, Oxalis acetosella, Shortia galacifolia;* **Pennie Logemann (courtesy of New England Wild Flower Society, Inc.):** *Aster cordifolius;* **Charles Mann:** *Antennaria parvifolia, Argemone hispida, Penstemon barbatus, Zinnia grandiflora;* **J. Paul Moore:** *Heuchera villosa;* **New England Wild Flower Society, Inc.:** *Nelumbo lutea;* **Steven Still:** *Allium cernuum, Campanula rotundifolia, Hesperis matronalis, Limnanthes douglasii, Polygonatum biflorum, Saponaria officinalis, Sedum spathulifolium;* **Michael S. Thompson:** *Geum triflorum, Iris versicolor.*